888.082
H125九

THREE GREE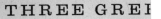

CHRISTIAN HERITAGE COLLEGE

CHRISTIAN
HERITAGE
COLLEGE
LIBRARY

PRESENTED BY

Dr. Donald L. Barbe

The Library of Liberal Arts

OSKAR PIEST, FOUNDER

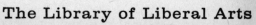
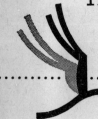

The Library of Liberal Arts

Hadas, Moses, 1900-   Ed. and tr.

→ THREE
GREEK
ROMANCES

Translated, with an Introduction, by
MOSES HADAS
Jay Professor of Greek, Columbia University

53-10378

The Library of Liberal Arts
published by
THE BOBBS-MERRILL COMPANY, INC.
A Subsidiary of Howard W. Sams & Co., Inc.
Publishers • Indianapolis • New York • Kansas City

About Longus and Xenophon of Ephesus, little is known. Longus probably lived at Lesbos during the third century A.D., and Xenophon of Ephesus during the second or third century A.D. Dio of Prusa (called Chrysostom, or Golden-Mouthed) was born in A.D. 40 and died in 120. He was a rhetor, and in 82 he was banished from Italy and for fourteen years led the life of a wandering Cynic preacher, remaining as an apostle of the Cynic-Stoic way of life after his recall from exile. His extant works include 80 orations and an essay, "Praise of Hair."

The Library of Liberal Arts edition
of THREE GREEK ROMANCES is published by agreement
with Doubleday & Company, Inc.

COPYRIGHT © 1953 by MOSES HADAS

THE BOBBS-MERRILL COMPANY, INC., 1964

Printed in the United States of America

Library of Congress Catalog Card Number 53—10378

First Printing

CONTENTS

26294

Introduction

"*Once upon a time*" *is not the way classical Greeks* opened a work of literature. When Solon retired from politics he went to see Thespis act a play, and was scandalized. "Are you not ashamed," said he to the playwright, "to tell so many lies before so many people?" Thespis replied that lies were legitimate in a work of the imagination, but Solon would not be convinced. Tragedians continued to write plays, but their personages and themes were derived from a body of myth which was regarded as ancient history; what they did, in effect, was to make the ancient histories intelligible and meaningful. Only the comic poets could freely invent persons and events, and the closest affinity of prose fiction, which is the latest literary invention of the Greeks, is with New Comedy.

From comedy the novel derived its love story, intrigue, recognition, and its bourgeois atmosphere, but the influence of other antecedent forms is equally apparent. The structure of the narrative, particularly in the longer novels, manifestly follows the pattern of the *Odyssey*. The idyllic atmosphere, most notable in *Daphnis and Chloe*, is a borrowing from pastoral poetry like Theocritus'. Characterization of bourgeois types through dialogue was a contribution of writers of mimes, who were significantly called "biologists," or students of life. Recurrent utopian elements were suggested by fanciful travel books, the aim of which was to point to improved political or social institutions. Rhetorical elements and ingeniously contrived situations came from the curricula of the schools. These include not only set apostrophes to or tirades against Fate, reflections on the paradoxes of Fortune, and the like, but also formal descriptions of works of art, exotic animals, royal courts, or picturesque landscapes.

So important is the rhetorical element in our novels that earlier students of the genre were convinced that it originated with the second-century-A.D. teachers of the so-called Second Sophistic. To afford their students material for verbal and casuistical acrobatics the rhetors proposed for discussion legal cases which are in effect skeleton plots for romances. A vestal convicted of violating her vow of virginity and flung down a precipice escapes without injury: should she be subjected to the ordeal a second time? Perhaps the gods wished to prolong her agony? Perhaps she had practiced falling down precipices in preparation? A man is captured by pirates but freed by the chief's daughter, whom he promises to marry; when he arrives home with his bride his father disinherits him. A loving couple vow not to survive each other; the husband sends the wife a false report of his death; the wife flings herself down a precipice but recovers; the father demands that she divorce him. Cases such as these (drawn from the elder Seneca's handbook on the subject) ultimately found their way into the *Gesta Romanorum* and thence into Boccaccio, from whom they were quarried by a thousand writers. Examples from a rhetorician's handbook readily evolve into stories. Erasmus wrote his *Colloquies* to supply students with useful Latin idioms, and from single sentences of specimen greetings appropriate to various occasions he proceeds by inevitable stages to longer pieces which are in effect short stories. These are not only entertaining, but give Erasmus' views on religion, literature, and politics.

Do our Greek novels too have aims beyond literary entertainment? To the classical Greeks the doctrine of art for art's sake would have appeared monstrous. Literature was an essential commodity, which like other commodities must be as aesthetically satisfying as expert craftsmanship could make it, but must also serve a useful purpose. The poet was recognized as a responsible teacher; instruction was not merely his privilege but his obligation. It was only in the Alexandrian age that exquisite form and abstruse erudition were pursued for their own sake, but even then the earlier Puritanical view of literature persisted, and even in the novel. It is not, to be sure, as easy to discern in the ancient as in the modern novel. Our own serious novels, like Attic tragedy, seek to establish or illustrate universal laws of human conduct or to promote certain moral attitudes. Both these motives are to be found in the Greek novel also, but their unfamiliar direction makes them hard to recognize, and their apparent absence has given these books an unfair reputation for frivolity.

What the serious reader finds most objectionable in the Greek novels is their shrieking implausibilities. There is no logic nexus between event and event or between event and character. But in a world where the links of causality are broken and Fortune has taken control of the affairs of men it is the very incalculability of events that absorbs interest. Logic is supplanted by paradox and emotion becomes sentimentality, to be savored for its own sake. The cavalier attitude to probability is not a mark of indifference but a true reflection of current beliefs. Consequently, by making virtue triumph in the end as they regularly do, our authors are consciously arguing that, appearances to the contrary notwithstanding, there *is* a divine power which does guide and protect its special charges. If *An Ephesian Tale* is an absorbing tale of love and improbable adventure, it is also a tract to prove that Diana of the Ephesians (who was equated with Isis) cares for her loyal devotees.

Apologetics for a cult, or more properly for the cultural minority who are its votaries, is probably the earliest motivation for the ancient novel. Descendants of proud peoples on the periphery of the Greek world who found themselves degraded as a result of Alexander's conquests glorified their past in romances in which their ancient national heroes were principal figures. In course of time the "historical" element in these tales receded and the erotic came to the fore, but the type continued to be used as an instrument for propaganda on behalf of rejected minorities or unpopular cults. Among extant novels the propaganda element is most important in Heliodorus' *Ethiopica,* but the author introduces his praise of the dark-skinned Ethiopians and of the Gymnosophist cult so skillfully as to make his motive unobtrusive. The Latin *Golden Ass* of Apuleius is clearly propaganda for the cult of Isis. In form *An Ephesian Tale* is a shorter parallel to the *Ethiopica*; in part, at least, it aims to justify the cult of Artemis-Isis.

Besides this major type of ancient prose romance two others are distinguishable by their special emphases—the pastoral and the utopian. Each of the three types contains elements of the other two, and all share certain common features. There are always hairbreadth escapes, separations, resounding triumphs against overwhelming temptations, miraculous reunions, sensational recognitions, shipwrecks, scenes in courts of law or of exotic potentates, and melodramatic endings where hero and heroine are vindicated before a large concourse of applauding spectators. Between the three types, however, the distinctions are clearly marked, as may be seen from the specimens of each presented in this volume.

    Far the best known of the three, and indeed the most widely admired work of all ancient fiction, is the *Daphnis and Chloe* of Longus. This is the perfect paradigm for the pastoral. The author advertises the artificiality of his work at once by describing it as the literary pendant of a painted picture. He is an urbane sophisticate writing for others of like taste. The influence of Theocritus is palpable, in names and incidents as well as atmosphere, and at the end of the third book an episode is introduced merely to provide explication for some familiar lines of Sappho:

Like the sweet apple which reddens upon the topmost bough,
A-top on the topmost twig—which the pluckers forgot, somehow—
Forgot it not, nay, but got it not, for none could get it till now.
                        (Translation of D. G. Rossetti)

The idyllic Arcady which the author of pastoral creates is a sort of laboratory, where external factors are controlled and the conduct of the unspoiled hero and heroine can be observed in isolation. Here they had been exposed in infancy, and here they are kept throughout the period relevant to the investigation. We can watch the untutored awakening and the progress of their love with understanding as well as sympathy. Disturbing influences—the experienced Lycainion, the brigands, the careless gallants—are intrusions from the outer world; we can watch the effect of each in the process of maturing. The isolation and the study is brought to an end by the arrival of Daphnis' true parents. After the hero and heroine's trials, and after their and the reader's education, they resume their proper place in society; but even so neither their nor, hopefully, the reader's life sinks back into conventional patterns.

The most closely packed of the romances proper is Xenophon's *An Ephesian Tale*. In astonishingly few pages we find strange journeys, shipwrecks, pirates and brigands, premature burials, incessant fruitless assaults on the virtue of both hero and heroine, and a final reunion against what seems to be overwhelming odds. Yet somehow the book succeeds in inducing a suspension of disbelief and even in winning sympathy not only for hero and heroine but also for the large cast of lesser characters. All are charitably conceived as human beings; brigands are good people fallen on hard times but still capable of generosity and loyalty, and even the bawd and slave dealer are kindly people who are only following their trade but whose sympathies can be engaged by a story of misfortune. The intending rapists are clearly helpless before the shattering beauty of their prospective victims. The macabre but bitter-sweet inset of Aigialeus and Thelxinoe is a minor masterpiece.

In Dio Chrysostom's *Hunters of Euboea* the laboratory aspects of the pastoral are as plainly marked as in *Daphnis and Chloe*. Here too the protagonists are impeccably virtuous, and here the utopian element is plainly uppermost and the romantic only a scaffolding. When the simple-minded and wholehearted rustic by his very naturalness outfaces the cunning city lawyer, the lesson of the corruption of civilization and of the nobility of the Cynic ideal of naturalness is eloquently enforced. The piece is in fact part of an "oration," the seventh of the eighty which Dio wrote.

Matrimony, not love, is the fulfillment of the prose romances. It is the goal of respectable marriage that gives breathlessness to the adventures which obstruct its consummation and happy release when it is in the end achieved. However high their birth, all that the protagonists desire is to settle down in secure and sober respectability, and this goal makes the atmosphere and character of the prose romances, however lurid their adventures, so like the bourgeois world of the New Comedy. There are no heroes in the classical sense, no towering figures like Achilles or Ajax so possessed by a code that loyalty to it must involve their death. Mere loyalty to a spouse could not, in epic or tragedy, be a sufficient object of heroism. By definition of the term, indeed, no man presumed to be living happily could be a hero. In one sense all of tragedy may be defined as a demonstration that the hero is in fact heroic, and, as in tragedy, all subsequent literary treatment of personages accepted as heroic was in poetry. The rule persisted throughout antiquity, though Alexandrian or Roman treatment of heroic saga might be pretty rather than profound. Jason in Apollonius of Rhodes's *Argonautica* is merely an inadequate hero, and Achilles in Quintus of Smyrna's *Posthomerica* is merely a sentimentalized hero. Both are shown to be in love, but love is only a sentimental adjunct to make them amiable, not the mainspring of their heroism. Love *is* the mainspring of Musaeus' poem on Hero and Leander, which restores the substance of the bourgeois novel to almost epic greatness. Authentic epic incidentally glorifies even such commonplaces of life as food and dress, but in Musaeus the glorification of love (not matrimony) is central, and love itself becomes an authentic object of nobility. Tristram and Launcelot follow in the path which Leander pioneered.

Besides the specimens presented in this volume, three other, and longer, examples of Greek prose romances have survived: Chariton's *Chaereas and Callirhoe*; Heliodorus' *Ethiopica* or *Theagenes and Charicleia*; and Achilles Tatius' *Clitophon and Leucippe*. Of none of these authors is anything positive known. The *Ecclesiastical History of Socrates* (sixth century A.D.) says that both Heliodorus and Achilles Tatius were bishops. There is no actual disproof of this statement, but it has been suggested that the episcopal title was attached to the names in order to make their books respectable reading for Byzantine monks, who were exceedingly fond of the novels and apparently had many more to read than the few which have survived. The evidence of a papyrus fragment indicates that Chariton wrote in the second century A.D.; Achilles Tatius may be as late as the fifth. Of the authors reprinted in this volume Xenophon, who is naturally not to be confused with the fourth-century-B.C. writer of that name, can hardly be earlier than the second century A.D. Longus belongs probably to the third century A.D. Dio is the only author in the present collection of whom other work is extant and whose dates are known. He came from Prusa in Asia Minor, and lived A.D. 40–120. As did the later Bishop of Constantinople, he received the surname "Golden-mouthed" (Chrysostom) for his eloquence. He was an earnest teacher in the Cynic-Stoic tradition, and in a sense a forerunner of Christian sermonizers. It may be noted in passing that Christians learned not only from pagan preachers but also from pagan romancers. The perfectly orthodox *Acts of Xanthippe and Polyxena,* first printed half a century ago and dated to the third or fourth century, has all the thrilling kidnapings, deliveries, and surprises of the typical Greek romance. The *Descent into Hell,* now embedded in the *Acts of Nicodemus,* is a vigorous and imaginative piece of fourth-century fiction and shows the effects of Greek models. Unlike their models these works have not, in recognizable form, entered the main stream of European literature. Here the influence of the Greek romances has not been as spectacular as that of epic or tragedy, but it has been nearly as strong and indeed more pervasive.

Daphnis and Chloe

BY LONGUS

Prologue

Once while I was hunting in Lesbos I saw in a grove of the Nymphs the fairest sight I have ever seen. It was the painted picture of a tale of love. The grove itself was beautiful; it was thick with trees, and abounding in flowers, all well-watered by a single fountain which brought refreshment to both alike. But more delightful still was that picture, both for its consummate art and for its tale of love. Its fame drew many visitors, even from a distance, to supplicate the Nymphs and to view the painting. In it were represented women in childbed, and others fitting swaddling clothes upon infants. There were sheep nursing them and shepherds taking them up; there were young lovers pledging faith to one another, an incursion of pirates, an attack by invaders. All these scenes spoke of love, and as I looked upon and admired them I conceived a strong desire to compose a literary pendant to that painted picture. Upon inquiry I found an interpreter of the picture, and I have carefully set the story out in four books, as an offering to Eros, the Nymphs, and Pan, and as a delightful possession for all mankind. It will remedy disease, solace grief, bring fond recollections to him that has loved, and instruct him that has not loved. None, indeed, has escaped love or ever shall, as long as beauty survives and eyes to see it. May the god vouchsafe me to retain prudence as I write of the vicissitudes of others.

1 *In Lesbos there is a large and handsome city, called* Mytilene. It is divided by canals into which the sea flows, and adorned with bridges of polished white stone. You would think it was no city you looked upon, but islands. At a distance of some two hundred furlongs from this city was the country property of a rich man, a very fair estate. Its mountains abounded with game, its fields with corn, its hills with vines, its pastures with herds. A wide beach of soft sand was formed by the sea which washed the shore.

On this estate a goatherd named Lamon tended goats, and there found an infant being suckled by a she-goat. The spot was an oak coppice and tangled thicket, with ivy winding about it and soft grass beneath; it was there the infant lay. To this coppice the goat would frequently run, and then disappear. To stay with the child, she would leave her own kid. Lamon watched her movements, being grieved to see the kid neglected, and when the sun was at its noonday heat he followed her footsteps. Her he saw standing over the infant with the utmost caution, to avoid treading upon it or hurting it with her hoofs, while the child, as if at its mother's breast, sucked greedy draughts of milk. To imagine Lamon's surprise is easy. He approached nearer and discovered a male child, big and fine, and wrapped in swaddling clothes better far than beseemed his castaway lot. He had a little mantle of fine purple, a golden brooch, and a tiny sword with an ivory hilt. Lamon's first thought was to appropriate the tokens and disregard the infant. But on reflection he was ashamed at conduct less humane than the goat's, and so he waited for night, when he fetched all to his wife Myrtale—the tokens, the child, and the she-goat too. Myrtale was astonished at the thought of goats producing little boys, but Lamon recounted his whole story: how he found it lying on the ground, how he saw it being suckled, and how he was overtaken with shame to leave it to perish. Myrtale shared his feelings, and so they hid the valuables, gave the child out as their own, and committed its nurture to the goat. And in order that the name of the child too should be suitably pastoral, they decided to call him Daphnis.

Now when two years had elapsed a shepherd of a neighboring pasturage, Dryas by name, chanced upon a similar find and a similar spectacle. There was a grotto of the Nymphs, a large rock, hollow within and curved without. In that grotto were statues of the Nymphs themselves, fashioned of stone. Their feet were unshod, their arms bare to the shoulders, their hair flowing loose upon their necks; on their hips they wore a girdle, and there was a smile upon their brows. Their whole appearance was of a choir dancing. The vault of the grotto rose over the center of the great rock, from which water bubbling formed a flowing stream. Before the cave there stretched a trim meadow of abundant soft grass fed by the fountain's moisture. Within the grotto hung milk pails, angular flutes, flageolets, and reed pipes, the dedications of the shepherds of old. To this grotto of the Nymphs a ewe newly lambed regularly resorted, so that more than once the shepherd supposed her lost. He wished to chastise her and reduce her to her former good behavior, and so twisted green osiers in the shape of a noose, and approached the rock with a view to laying hold of her. But on his arrival a far different sight than he had expected greeted him. His ewe he found affectionately offering copious draughts of milk from her udder to an infant; the infant, for its part, eagerly turned its face, clean and shining, from one teat to the other, uttering never a cry; and after it had drawn its fill the ewe licked the child's face with its tongue. This time it was a girl, and by it too there lay swaddling clothes, and trinkets—a headband of gold, gilt shoes, and golden anklets. Heaven-sent did Dryas consider his find, and, learning from the sheep her lesson of compassion and parental love, he took the infant up into his arms, laid its tokens by in his scrip, and prayed the Nymphs for good hap in rearing their suppliant. And when it came time to fold his flock, he returned to his steading, recounted to his wife the sights he had seen, and showed her the trove he had found. He bade her accept the babe as her own little girl, and so to rear it, keeping its origin secret. So then Nape (for so was she called) at once became the mother and loved the child tenderly, as if she was afraid of being outdone by the ewe. To lend her motherhood credit, she too gave the child a pastoral name—Chloe.

Both children grew rapidly, and revealed a beauty more exquisite than became rustics. The lad was now turned fifteen and the lass two years his junior when, in the same night Dryas and Lamon saw a dream somewhat as follows: it seemed that those Nymphs of the grotto with the fountain, in which Dryas had found the babe, handed over both Daphnis and Chloe to a pert and pretty boy who had wings on his shoulders and carried a little bow and arrows in his hand. This boy then touched the lad and lass with a single arrow and enjoined them to follow a pastoral life, he to tend goats and she to tend sheep. When their foster parents saw this dream they were distressed to think the children would be but shepherds. From their fine swaddling clothes they had fancied a better fortune for them, and therefore had provided them better fare and taught them their letters and such other matters as rustics understand. Yet they considered that since the children had been preserved by divine providence, the divine behests must be heeded. And so, when they had communicated the dream to one another and had offered sacrifice to the Winged Boy, Companion of the Nymphs (his true name they did not know), they instructed the twain in their duties as shepherds and sent them out with the flocks. They learned how to pasture their herds before the noonday heat, and how when its intensity was abated, when to take them to water, and when to return them to the fold, which of their charges required the crook, and for which the voice alone was sufficient. They were exceedingly happy with their charge, as if it were some high ministry, and they loved their sheep and goats more than is common among shepherds—Chloe, because she owed her salvation to a ewe, and Daphnis, because he remembered that it was a goat who suckled him when he lay helpless.

The spring was at its prime and everywhere flowers were in bloom, in the woods, in the meadows, on the hills. Now was there buzzing of bees, warbling of songbirds, frolicking of lambs; on the hillsides the flocks gamboled, the bees went humming through the meadows, and through the thickets the birds made minstrelsy. And when such springtide joy held everything in thrall, the young and tender pair imitated all they heard and all they saw. When they heard the caroling of the birds they too burst into song; when they saw the sportive lambs they too skipped lightly about; and the bees they imitated by gathering flowers. With some they filled their bosoms, others they wreathed into garlands and bestowed upon the Nymphs. All their work they did together, and they tended their flocks nigh one another. Often would Daphnis restore her sheep that had strayed, and often would Chloe drive his too venturesome goats from a precipice. Occasionally one would take charge of both flocks while the other was intent upon some pastime. Their amusements were of a childish and pastoral kind. Chloe would go hunting asphodel stalks, of which she wove traps for grasshoppers, neglecting her flock the while. Daphnis cut slender reeds, perforated the intervals between the joints, fitted them together with soft wax, and then practiced piping till nightfall. Sometimes they shared their milk and wine, and made a common meal of the provisions they brought from home. Sooner would one see the flocks of sheep or goats separated from one another than Daphnis and Chloe apart.

Now while they were passing their time in such amusements, Eros contrived trouble for them. A she-wolf from the adjoining countryside harried the flocks because she required food for her large litter. The villagers gathered by night and dug pits a yard wide and four deep. Most of the earth which they dug out they carried to a distance and scattered; the rest they spread over long dry sticks which they laid across the opening, so as to resemble the former appearance of the spot. The sticks were weaker than straws, so that if even a hare ran over them they would break; but only then would one know that this was not solid earth but only an imitation of it. Many such pits they dug, both in the hills and on the plain, but the wolf they never succeeded in capturing, for she perceived the deception. But their advice did cost them many sheep and goats, and almost, as we shall see, Daphnis himself. Two goats fell into a temper and started to fight, and when their butting grew violent the horn of one was broken, and he ran off, bellowing with pain. The victor followed at his heels in hot pursuit. Daphnis was vexed at the broken horn and at the truculence of the aggressor, and so seized his crook and pursued the pursuer. The one thus flying and the other passionate in his chase, neither saw clearly what lay at their feet, and so both tumbled into the pit, the goat first and Daphnis after him. This, in fact, is what saved Daphnis, for he used the goat as a mount in his fall. There was Daphnis in tears, hoping for someone to pass and pull him out. Chloe saw what had happened and came flying to the pit, and when she found that he was alive, called a cowherd from a nearby field to come and help. The cowherd came, and looked about for a long rope by which Daphnis could be pulled out, but none was to be found. Thereupon Chloe undid her band and gave it to the cowherd to let down. And so they took a stand at the rim of the pit and pulled, and Daphnis emerged clutching the band with his hands. They also pulled out that wretched goat, who now had both horns broken, the vanquished being soon avenged, and gave him, as recompense for his share in saving Daphnis, to the cowherd to offer as sacrifice. If any at home should miss the goat they were prepared to pretend that a wolf had attacked it. Then they went back to examine their flocks, and when they found that both the goats and the sheep were grazing quietly and undisturbed, they sat down at the stump of an oak and scrutinized Daphnis' body to see whether any part of it had been bloodied in the fall. No hurt or blood was to be seen, but his hair and the rest of his body were plastered with mud and dirt; to conceal the mischance from Lamon and Myrtale, he resolved to wash himself. With Chloe, then, he went to the grotto of the Nymphs, and gave her his tunic and scrip to hold while he stood by the fountain and washed his hair and all his body. Now his hair was black and full, and his body tinted by the sun; one might suppose it took its color from the shadow of his hair. Chloe looked on and thought him beautiful, and, having never thought him beautiful before, she thought that the bath was what conferred beauty. As she washed his back and shoulders his soft flesh yielded to her touch and she privily touched her own flesh to try whether she were the more tender. For the time, then, since the sun was at its setting, they drove their flocks

8   *Daphnis and Chloe*

home; and Chloe felt no other sensation except that she mightily desired to see Daphnis at his bathing again.

On the following day, when they reached their pasturage, Daphnis sat under his usual oak and played on his pipe, the while watching his goats, who seemed to take pleasure in the music. Chloe sat nearby and looked, indeed, at her flock of sheep, but much more did she look at Daphnis, and again she found him beautiful as he piped. Now she thought it was the music that produced beauty, so she took the pipe up after him, that she too might become beautiful. Then she persuaded him to bathe again, and she watched him as he bathed, and touched him as she watched. She went home filled with praise of him, and that praise was the beginning of love. What had come over her she did not know, being but a young girl and country bred and never having so much as heard the word "love" pronounced. But restlessness governed her spirit, she could not control her eyes, and frequently she murmured, "Daphnis." She neglected her food, lay awake at night, was unheeding of her flock. She laughed and wept by turns; now she would doze off, now start up; her face turned pale, and again burned with hot blushes. Not even a cow stung by a horsefly behaves so skittish. In a reverie she reasoned with herself as follows:

"I am sick for sure, but what the malady is I do not know. I am in pain, but can find no bruise. I am distressed, yet none of my sheep is missing. I feel a burning, yet am sitting in thick shade. How many times have I been pricked by brambles, yet I never cried; how many times have bees stung me, but I never lost my appetite. The thing that pricks my heart now is sharper than those. Daphnis is beautiful, but so are the flowers; his pipe makes fine music, but so does the nightingale—but flowers and nightingales do not disturb me. Would I could become a pipe, so that he might breathe upon me, a goat, that I might graze in his care! Ah, cruel water! Only Daphnis did you make beautiful; my bathing was useless. I perish, dear Nymphs, and you do nothing to save the maiden who grew up among you. Who will crown you with flowers after I am gone? Who will take care of my poor lambs? Who will tend my chirping cicada? It cost me much trouble to catch, so that its song might lull me to sleep in the grotto; but now I cannot sleep because of Daphnis, and its chirping is useless!"

Such were her sufferings, such her discourse, as she groped for the name of love. Now Dorcon, that cowherd who had raised Daphnis and the goat out of the pit, was a brisk young fellow, newly bearded, who knew not only the name but the facts of love, and from that very day he was smitten with Chloe. As time went on his spirit became more inflamed, and, despising Daphnis as a mere child, he determined to work his will either by gifts or by force. At first he brought them both presents, for Daphnis a shepherd's pipe with its nine reeds fastened with bronze instead of wax, for her a spotted bacchic fawn skin, its color as if it were painted with various tinges. Being accounted their friend in consequence, he gradually neglected Daphnis, but every day brought something to Chloe—a delicate cheese, a nosegay, a ripe apple. Once he brought her a newborn calf, and a gilt ivy cup, and fledglings of a wild bird. Having no experience of a lover's wiles, she received the gifts very gladly, pleased to have the wherewithal to give Daphnis pleasure. But now it was time for Daphnis too to know the effects of love, and he and Dorcon fell into a dispute concerning their respective beauty. Chloe was the umpire, and the victor's prize was to kiss Chloe. Dorcon was the first, and spoke as follows:

"I, my girl, am bigger than Daphnis, and I am a cowherd while he is a goatherd; I am, therefore, as much better than he as cows are than goats. Moreover I am as white as milk, and my hair is red like grain ready for the harvest; I was brought up by a mother, not an animal. That fellow is puny, unbearded like a woman, and black like a wolf. He keeps goats and reeks of their stench. He is so poor that he cannot keep even a dog. If it is true, as they say, that a nanny gave him suck, he is no better than a goat."

Such and the like were Dorcon's words, and after him Daphnis spoke: "True, I was suckled by a goat; so was Zeus. The goats I keep are bigger than his cows. I smell of them no more than does Pan, who is himself mostly goat. I am content with cheese and johnnycake and sweet wine—wealth enough for a shepherd. I am beardless, true, but so is Dionysus; dark, but so is the hyacinth; but Dionysus is better than satyrs, and the hyacinth than lilies. This fellow is red like a fox, and bearded like a goat, and white like a city wench. If you must kiss, it is my mouth you can kiss, but only bristles on his chin. And remember, girl, that you too were nursed by an animal, but still you are beautiful."

Chloe waited no longer, but partly out of pleasure at his praise and partly because she had long yearned to kiss Daphnis, she leapt up and gave him the prize, an artless and unsophisticated kiss, to be sure, but sufficient to set his heart on fire. Dorcon was much vexed, and went off to seek some other way of wooing. But Daphnis, as if he had been bitten rather than kissed, suddenly became gravity itself; he shivered by fits, and could not control his palpitating heart. He wanted to look at Chloe, but when he looked he was suffused with blushes. Then for the first time did he admire her hair because it was yellow, and her eyes, because they were big and soft like a heifer's, and her face, because it was truly whiter than his own goats' milk. It was as if he then first acquired eyes, having had none before. Now he took no food more than a morsel to taste, no drink except to wet his lips, and that under compulsion. Now was he fallen silent, who had been more chattering than the crickets, now sluggish, who had been brisker than a goat. His flock was neglected, his pipes flung away. His face was paler than summer grass. To Chloe alone was he talkative, and if ever he was away from her he would spin such fond soliloquies as this:

"What in the world has Chloe's kiss done to me? Her lips are softer than rose petals, her mouth sweeter than honeycomb; and yet that kiss was sharper than a bee's sting. Often have I kissed kids, often have I kissed young puppies, and the calf which Dorcon gave me. But this is a new kind of kiss. My breath leaps out, my heart jumps about, my spirit melts—and yet I want to be kissed again! Ah, that bad victory; ah, that novel malady, of which I do not even know how to say the name! Can it be that Chloe tasted some poison when she was going to kiss me? Then why did she not die? How cheerily the nightingales sing—but my pipe is silent; how gaily the kids gambol—and I sit listless; how richly the flowers bloom—and I weave no garlands; the violets and hyacinths are in flower, but Daphnis droops and withers. Shall Dorcon be looked upon as handsomer than me?" Such things did our excellent Daphnis suffer and such things did he say, when he first tasted the effects and the language of love.

But Dorcon, that cowherd who was in love with Chloe, watched his chance, and when Dryas was digging his vines nearby he approached him with some handsome cheeses. These he bestows as a gift from an old acquaintance and colleague, and with such an introduction broached the subject of marriage. If he could take Chloe to wife he promised many fine gifts, such as a cowherd could afford—a team of plow oxen, four swarms of bees, fifty apple seedlings, an oxhide for making shoes, a weaned calf every year. It wanted but little for Dryas, who was tempted by these gifts, to give his assent to the marriage. But then he bethought him that the girl deserved a better match; he was afraid the girl's origin would one day be discovered and he find himself in great trouble for bartering her away. And so he asked Dorcon's pardon for rejecting his inventory of gifts, and refused his offer.

Now when Dorcon had failed in his second hope and had lost his good cheeses in vain, he determined to lay hands on Chloe when he should find her alone. He kept watch and noticed that Daphnis and the girl took their flocks to water on alternate days, and so contrived a scheme worthy of a cowherd. He took the skin of a big wolf, whom a bull defending his cows had killed with his horns, and drew it over his body, from his shoulder's down to his feet, fitting the forepaws over his hands and the back paws over his legs down to his heels. The mane of the wolf covered his head like an infantryman's helmet. Having made so perfect a beast of himself as was possible, he approached the spring where the goats and sheep drank after their grazing. The spring lay in a hollow, and all the region around grew wild with brambles and briars and juniper and thistles; a real wolf would likely choose such a spot for his lair. There Dorcon hid himself and waited for the cattle to be watered, in high hopes that his disguise would terrify Chloe and bring her into his power.

Nor had he long to wait. Chloe came driving the flock to the spring, having left Daphnis behind cutting green leaves to feed the kids after their grass. The dogs who helped guard her cattle followed, sniffing busily about as is their way, and discovered Dorcon crawling forward to attack the girl. Taking him for a wolf, they burst into full cry and set upon him. They surrounded him, and before he could recover from his astonishment, sank their teeth through the skin. He was ashamed of being discovered and was protected by the covering of skin, and so for a time remained quiet where he lurked. But in her alarm at the sight Chloe called Daphnis to help, and when the dogs had pulled off the skin and were now snapping at his flesh, Dorcon bellowed in pain, and called upon Chloe and Daphnis (who was now come) to help him. The dogs they quickly gentled with their accustomed call; but Dorcon, who was bitten on the thighs and shoulders, they carried to the spring. There they washed off the wounds where the marks of the dogs' teeth showed, and plastered them with green elm's bark which they had softened by chewing. So innocent were they of the desperate ventures lovers undertake that they thought Dorcon's disguise was some shepherd's trick, and so far from being angry they even comforted him. When they had helped him along on their arms for some distance they sent him off. So Dorcon, who had escaped so great a danger and had been preserved not, as he would likely say, from the mouth of a wolf, but from that of a dog, nursed his wounds.

But Daphnis and Chloe had much trouble, before nightfall, collecting their goats and sheep. These had been terrified by the wolf's skin and confused by the yelping of the dogs, and some ran up the cliffs and others down to the very sea. They had been trained, indeed, to heed a call, and to be soothed by notes of the pipe, and to assemble at clapping of hands; but terror made them forget all their training, and Daphnis and Chloe had much ado to find them. They tracked them down like hares, and at last brought them to their steadings. That night alone they enjoyed a profound sleep, weariness providing a drug for their lovers' distress. But with the coming of day their passion awoke in them again—the pleasure of meeting at dawn; the sorrow of parting at dusk. They wanted something, but knew not what they wanted; this only they knew, that the one had perished of a kiss, and the other of a bath.

The season of the year added fuel to their fire. Now spring was ended and summer begun, and all things were at their prime: the trees were laden with fruit, the fields with grain. Pleasant was the chirping of the crickets, sweet the aroma of fruit, delightful the bleating of lambs. One might fancy that even the rivers in their gentle course murmured soft music, that the breezes piped when they breathed upon the pines, that apples fell to earth out of love, and that the sun, who was a lover of beauty, stripped all things of their coverings. All these things warmed Daphnis, and he plunged into the rivers; sometimes he bathed, and sometimes he chased the fish that swirled about in the water; sometimes he drank deeply, as if to quench the fire within. Chloe, for her part, after she had milked the ewes and also many of the goats, had much trouble thickening her cream, for the flies vexed her and would sting if she tried to drive them off. But afterwards she washed her face, put on a garland of pine twigs, girt herself in her fawn skin, and filled a piggin with wine and milk to share with Daphnis. But when noon came on, their eyes succumbed to ravishment. For when Chloe looked upon Daphnis nude, his beauty smote her in a mass, and she melted, and could find fault with no part of him. And when Daphnis saw her in fawn skin and pine wreath holding the piggin out to him, he thought it was one of the Nymphs of the grotto he beheld. The pine, then, he snatched from her head, and crowned his own with it, first covering the wreath with kisses. And when he stripped for his bath, she dressed herself in his garment, having kissed that. Sometimes they pelted each other with apples, and dressed each other's hair, dividing the locks. She likened his hair to myrtle, because it was dark; and he her face to an apple, because it was fair with ruddy tinge. He would teach her, too, to pipe, and when she began to breathe into the instrument, would snatch it from her and run over the reeds with his own lips; he seemed to be correcting her fault, but was bestowing decent kisses on Chloe by means of the pipe.

Once he was piping at midday and his beasts were lying in the shade, Chloe imperceptibly dozed off. Daphnis noticed, and, laying his pipe aside, gazed upon her insatiably, for there was none to shame him, and gently he murmured, "What eyes are those that slumber, what a mouth that breathes so sweet! No apples are like it, no flowering shrubs. But to kiss her I dread; her kiss stings to the heart, and like new honey causes madness. I am afraid too that my kiss may rouse her from sleep. Ah, those chattering crickets! Their shrill din will not let her sleep. And those goats too are crashing their horns, butting one another. The wolves must have turned more craven than foxes not to ravage them!" While he indulged in such discourse a cricket avoiding a swallow which was chasing it took refuge in Chloe's bosom. The pursuing swallow could not now reach her prey, but the chase brought her near to Chloe, whose cheeks were brushed by her wings. Not knowing what was happening, Chloe screamed and started up from her sleep. But when she saw the swallow fluttering nearby and Daphnis laughing at her alarm, her fear vanished, and she fell to rubbing her eyes, which still craved sleep. Now the cricket chirped from out of her bosom, like a suppliant rendering thanks for its safety. Again Chloe screamed and Daphnis laughed. Seizing the pretext, he thrust his hands down to her breast and brought out that noble cricket, which refused to be silent even in his right hand. Chloe was pleased at sight of the creature, and took it in her hand and kissed it, and then put it back into her bosom, still chirping.

Once they were entertained by a ringdove sounding its pastoral note from the forest. Chloe asked what the song meant, and Daphnis told her an old country tale:

"Once, my girl, there was a beautiful girl like you; she was your age, and tended cattle in the forest. She was very musical too, and the cattle were charmed by her song, so that she needed no blow of the crook or thrust of the goad to manage them. She would sit under a pine and wear a wreath of pine twigs and sing of Pan and the Nymph, Pitys, and the cows would hearken to her singing. A lad who kept cows at no great distance, himself handsome and musical like the girl, vied with her in singing; being a man, his tones were fuller, and being young, sweeter. Thus he charmed away to his own herd eight of her best cows. The maiden was mortified at losing her cattle and being worsted in song, and she prayed the gods to be transformed into a bird before she reached home. The gods heeded her prayer and made of her this bird, like the maiden a mountain dweller, and like her tuneful. Even now her song bespeaks her misfortune, for it is of one seeking cattle that have strayed."

Such were the pleasures that summer afforded them. When autumn came and grapes were ripening, certain Tyrian pirates using a Carian barque (not to appear barbarians) made land at that coast. They made a descent armed in half corselets and with sword in hand, and swept away everything they encountered—fragrant wine, quantities of wheat, honey in the comb, and they also drove off some cows from Dorcon's herd. And they also seized Daphnis, who was rambling down by the sea. Chloe took Dryas' flocks out rather late, for, being a girl, she was timid before the saucy shepherds. When the pirates saw the tall and handsome youth, who was a better prize than their plunder from the fields, they took no more trouble about the goats, nor did they go farther afield, but hurried him to their ship, weeping, helpless, and calling loudly upon Chloe. But the pirates slipped their cable, put their hands to the oars, and made the high sea. By now Chloe was driving her flock out, and carrying a new pipe as a gift for Daphnis. She saw Daphnis' goats all in confusion, and heard himself shouting for her ever more loudly. She quitted her sheep, threw down the pipe, and ran towards Dorcon to implore his help. Dorcon had been slashed down to earth by the vigorous strokes of the pirates; he still breathed a little, but was streaming with blood. But when he saw Chloe he caught a spark of his former love, and said, "In just a little, Chloe, I shall die; those accursed pirates have cut me down like an ox, as I was fighting to save my cows. Do you now save Daphnis, and avenge me, and destroy those rogues. I have trained those cows to heed the sound of my pipe and to follow its sound even if they should be grazing at a great distance. Come, then, take this pipe and blow on it the tune which I once taught Daphnis and Daphnis you. Leave the rest to the pipe and the cows out yonder. The pipe itself I give you as a present; with it I won many a contest with cowherds and goatherds. In return for all this give me but a kiss while I am yet alive, and shed a tear for me when I am dead. And when you see another tending my cows, think of Dorcon."

So much Dorcon said, and kissed his last kiss; with the kiss and his voice he yielded up his life. But Chloe took the pipe and put it to her lips and piped as loudly as she could. The cows heard the melody and recognized it; with a single impulse they began to low and jumped into the sea. By the violence of their spring to the same side of the ship and of their leap, a great chasm yawned in the sea; the ship overturned, and, when the waves poured in, foundered. Those in the vessel tumbled into the sea, but not all with the same hope of reaching the shore. The pirates were encumbered by swords, weighed down with scaled corselets, and constricted by greaves which reached to midleg: whereas Daphnis was barefoot, for he had been grazing in the plain, and half naked, for the weather was still hot. The pirates, then, swam for a little, but their armor bore them down to the abyss; Daphnis easily stripped his garment off, but swam with difficulty, for before then he had swum only in rivers. Finally, necessity teaching him what he must do, he thrust himself into the midst of the cows, and seizing the horns of two cows in his two hands, he was carried along as easily and securely as if he were riding in a wagon. Your ox, you must know, swims better than a man; he is surpassed only by waterfowl and, of course, by fish. An ox is never in danger of drowning, unless his hoofs become softened by the water and drop off. This is corroborated by the many places in the sea which to this day bear the name Ox-ford.

In this way was Daphnis saved, escaping two evils beyond all hope, pirates and shipwreck. When he emerged from the sea he found Chloe on the shore, laughing and crying at once. He fell onto her bosom, and asked why she had chosen to pipe that melody. She told him the whole story—her running to Dorcon, the training of his cattle, her being bidden to pipe, his death; only the kiss she did not mention, out of shame. They resolved to honor their benefactor, and so they came, along with his kindred, and buried poor Dorcon. Then they heaped a mound of earth over his grave, and planted it with various trees, and hung up the first fruits of their labors. They also poured libations of milk, crushed grapes over the tomb, and broke many shepherd's pipes upon it. There was heard, too, the pitiful lowing of cattle, and uneasy movements were observed to attend the lowing. Among the shepherds and goatherds it was conjectured that this was the lamentation of the cattle for their deceased cowherd.

After the burial of Dorcon, Chloe took Daphnis to the Nymphs, and brought him into the grotto, and there bathed him. And she herself then for the first time bathed her body in the sight of Daphnis. White it was and pure in its beauty, and needed no bathing to make it beautiful. Then they gathered flowers, such blooms as that season afforded, and they crowned the statues, and hung Dorcon's pipe on the rock as a votive offering. After this they returned to inspect their goats and sheep. All were lying down, neither grazing nor bleating, but longing, I must think, for Daphnis and Chloe to reappear. And so when they came into sight and gave their customary call and sounded their pipes, the sheep got up and began to feed and the goats bounded about in their gambols, as if they were overjoyed by the deliverance of their accustomed goatherd.

But Daphnis could not persuade his soul to rejoice, now that he had seen Chloe nude and the beauties formerly concealed uncovered. Pain gnawed at his heart, as if he were being consumed by drugs. His breath was now panting, as if someone were pursuing him, and now failed altogether, as though it had been exhausted with his running. That bath seemed to him to be a more fearful thing than the sea. His soul, he thought, was still tarrying with the pirates; for he was young, and a rustic, and so far ignorant of the piratical ways of love.

2 *And now when autumn too was full-blown and the* season of vintage was at hand, everyone was busy at his rural tasks. One prepared the wine presses, another cleansed the tuns, another twisted osiers into baskets. One was charged with providing short pruning hooks for cutting the clusters, another a heavy stone capable of crushing the teeming grapes, another

vine branches beaten to a tinder to furnish light for drawing off the must at night. In this busy season Daphnis and Chloe neglected their sheep and goats, and each lent a hand to the other's tasks. Daphnis carried the clusters in baskets, threw them into the presses and trod them, and drew off the wine into casks. Chloe prepared food for the vintagers, poured old wine for their drink, and plucked off the bunches of grapes that hung low. Indeed, all the grapevines of Lesbos are of low growth; instead of shooting upward or trailing up trees, they spread their tendrils downwards and trail like ivy, so that even a child whose hands have just been loosed out of his swaddling bands might reach the grapes.

As was customary at the festival of Dionysus and the birth of wine, the women from the neighboring countryside were called in to help. These cast their eyes upon Daphnis and praised his beauty as being like that of Dionysus. One bold wench even kissed Daphnis, which set him aflame but vexed poor Chloe. On the other hand, the men at the wine press flung various remarks at Chloe, and, like satyrs around a bacchant, they leapt about her madly and vowed they'd become sheep and be tended by her; this, in turn, pleased Chloe but tormented Daphnis. Each of them wished the vintage would quickly be finished, so they could resume their customary haunts, and instead of the unharmonious shouting hear again the sound of their pipes and of their bleating flocks. And in a few days the vines were indeed stripped and the tuns filled with must, and there was no longer need of extra hands: and so they drove their herds to the plain. Filled with joy, they paid obeisance to the Nymphs, and brought them clusters still on their vine branches as first fruits of the vintage. Nor had they ever passed the grotto in time past with indifference, but always at the beginning of their pasturing they saluted the Nymphs, and on their return in the evening bowed down to them. And always they brought some offering—either a flower, or fruit, or a green leaf, or a libation of milk. And in time to come they received due requital from the deities. But on that occasion they were like dogs, as they say, loosed from the leash: they frolicked and piped and sang and playfully wrestled with their goats and sheep.

While they were thus gaily taking their pleasure, there approached an old man clothed in a rough cloak, shod with undressed leather, and carrying a scrip—a very old scrip—at his back. This man took a seat near them and spoke as follows: "I am old man Philetas, my children. Many songs have I sung to these Nymphs here, many times have I piped to yonder Pan, and many a herd of cows have I guided by my music alone. I am come to inform you of what I have seen, to report what I have heard. I have a garden which I have worked with my own hands from the time that old age stopped my herding. Whatever the seasons bring my garden produces. In the spring it has roses, lilies, and hyacinth, and both kinds of violets; in the summer poppies and pears and all varieties of apple; now it has vines and figs and pomegranates and green myrtles. To this garden troops of birds make their way together each morning, some for food and some to sing, for it is overarched and shady and abundantly watered by three springs; if one would remove its hedge he would fancy he was looking at a natural wood.

"When I entered my garden about noon today I espied a little boy under my pomegranates and myrtles, some of which he was holding in his hands. His complexion was as white as milk, his hair bright as fire, and he shone as if he had just been bathing. He was naked and alone, and he was playing as if it was his own garden he was culling. I started for him, to lay hands on him, for I was afraid that in his wantonness he might break my myrtles and pomegranates; but lightly and easily did he evade me, sometimes scampering under the rosebushes, and again snuggling under the poppies, like a fledgling partridge. Often in the past had I had my troubles in chasing nursling kids, frequently I winded myself running after newborn calves; but this was a mercurial creature and utterly elusive. I soon wearied, being as I am an old man, and so I leaned on my stick, keeping him under my eye so that he should not fly, and I asked to which of my neighbors he belonged, and what he meant by culling another's garden. He made no answer at all, but approached with a most winning smile, and pelted me with myrtle berries and in some mysterious way charmed away all my anger. I begged him to come where I could touch him, assuring him he need have no more fear, and I swore by the myrtles that I would let him go, and that I would give him apples and pomegranates in addition, and permission at any time to gather as much fruit and pluck as many flowers as he wished, if only I could obtain a single kiss from him.

"Thereupon he burst into a gay peal of laughter, and his utterance was more charming than a swallow's, than a nightingale's, than a swan's when it has grown old like me: 'I do not in the least grudge you a kiss, Philetas, for I take greater pleasure in being kissed than you would in recovering your youth; but consider whether the gift is appropriate to your time of life. After a single kiss old age will not avail to prevent you from pursuing me further. But I am very hard to catch, and swifter than a hawk or eagle or other bird of prey. Nor am I a child even if I seem to be one; I am older than Kronos and than Time himself. I knew you well in your early manhood when you tended your straggling herd on yonder mountain, and I sat by your side when you piped 'neath yonder beeches and were in love with Amaryllis. But you did not see me though I stood very near the girl. Her I gave to you, and now you have sons, good cowherds and farmers. Now I am shepherding Daphnis and Chloe, and when I have brought them together of a morning I come to your garden and take my pleasure in the flowers and the fruit, and bathe in these fountains. That is why your flowers and fruits are so beautiful: they are irrigated by my bath water. See whether any of your plants is crushed, if any fruit is plucked, if any flower stems are trodden down, if any spring is fouled!— and rejoice that you alone of mankind have in your old age beheld this boy.'

"When he had so spoken he leapt among the myrtles like a youngling nightingale, scampered from one bough to another, and through the leaves ascended to the very top. I caught a glimpse of wings sprouting from his shoulders, and a little bow and arrow between his wings and his shoulders; but then I saw neither them nor him. If I have not grown these gray hairs in vain, if old age has not made me a dotard, you, my children, are consecrated to Eros, and Eros has care of you."

Daphnis and Chloe were entranced with the story, but took

it as a fairy tale and not as a rational argument. They asked who this Eros was, whether a boy or a bird, and what his powers might be. Then Philetas spoke again: "A god is Eros, my children, young and handsome and winged. Therefore does he take pleasure in youth, and he pursues beauty and he endows souls with wings. He possesses greater power than Zeus himself. He rules the elements, he rules the stars, he rules his fellow deities; your power over your goats and sheep is not as great. All flowers are the work of Eros, all these plants are his handiwork; it is through him that rivers flow and breezes blow. I myself have seen a bull in love, and he bellowed as if stung by a horsefly; I have seen a goat in love, and he followed his she-goat everywhere. I myself was once young and in love with Amaryllis, and I forgot my food, and took no drink, and had no sleep. My soul fell sick, my heart palpitated, my body shivered. I cried out as one beaten, I fell dumb like a corpse, I plunged into the rivers like a man on fire. I called on Pan to help me, for he had himself loved Pitys. I thanked Echo for pronouncing Amaryllis' name after me. I broke my pipes, for though they soothed my cows they could not bring my Amaryllis. There is no drug for Eros—nothing to drink or to swallow and no spells to chant—but only kisses and embraces and lying together with naked bodies."

When he had thus instructed them Philetas departed, having received for his tuition sundry cheeses and a kid with burgeoning horns. And now that they were left by themselves, what they heard of Eros caused their spirits to shrink in distress; and at night, when they returned to their steadings, they compared their own sensations with what they had heard: "Lovers are sad; so are we sad. They neglect their food; so have we neglected ours. They are unable to sleep; that is precisely our experience also. They seem to be on fire; we too seem to burn. They are eager to see one another; that is the reason we pray for the day to come quickly. Perhaps this is love, and we are in love with one another without knowing it, and I am actually loved. Why else are we sad? Why do we always seek one another? All that Philetas said is true. That boy in the garden is the same one who appeared to our fathers in that dream and bade us become shepherds. But how can anyone catch him? He is little and will elude us. And how can one escape him? He has wings, and can overtake us. We must have recourse to the Nymphs to help us. Yet Pan did not help Philetas when he was in love with Amaryllis. It is the drugs the old man spoke of that we must seek—kisses and embraces and lying naked on the ground. It is very cold, but we can endure what Philetas could endure."

Thus they reviewed their lesson during the night. On the following day, when they led their flocks out to pasture, upon seeing one another they kissed, which they had never done before, and threw their arms about one another and embraced. The third remedy, stripping and lying down, they shrank from; it was too bold a step, not only for a girl, but for a young goatherd. Again night brought sleeplessness and reflection on what had taken place and regret for what had been omitted. "We kissed one another, but that was no help; we embraced one another, but that brought no relief. It must be that lying together is the only remedy for love, and so we must try that. That must have greater efficacy than a kiss." Their reflections being of such a nature, it was natural that love should occupy their dreams also, and they dreamt of kisses and embraces; and what they had failed to do by day they did in their dreams, and lay with one another on the ground naked. With spirits more agitated they arose the following morning, and drove their flocks briskly down, for they were eagerly hurrying to their kisses. And when they caught sight of one another they ran forward with beaming faces. There quickly followed kisses and close embraces, but the third remedy was slow in coming, for neither had Daphnis the boldness to speak, nor did Chloe wish to make the beginning, until chance brought them to do their will. They were sitting under an oak trunk, close by one another, and, having tasted the delight of kissing, were insatiably straining to get their fill of the pleasure. They threw their arms about one another to press their lips tighter together. When Daphnis hugged Chloe close and strained her body to his she fell over on her side, and he followed her with his close kiss. They recognized the figure of their dream, and for a long while lay locked in each other's arms as if enchanted. What came next they knew not, and thought this was the limit of the pleasures of love. In vain then did they squander the greater part of that day, and they drove their flocks home loathing the approach of night. Perhaps they might have achieved the true enjoyment of love had not the following disturbance set the whole countryside in confusion.

Some rich young gallants of Methymna had decided to celebrate the vintage in a new place, and so they launched a small ship and embarked their servants as rowers and sailed toward the fields of Mytilene which lie by the sea. The shore afforded safe harborage and was studded with fine houses; there were many baths and gardens and groves, some the works of nature, others of human artifice, but all suitable for youthful pleasures. Here they landed and moored their vessel. They did no mischief, but amused themselves with various sports. Some with hooks attached to reed canes by a thin line fished for rockfish from a promontory; others with dogs and nets hunted the hares who fled from the noises of the vintagers. Some went after birds and set snares for wild geese, ducks, and bustards, so that their sport supplied the needs of their table. When they needed anything more they obtained it from the farmers, and paid more than the fair value. Bread, wine, and shelter were all they needed, for they did not think it safe, with fall weather coming on, to spend the night at sea, and so, for fear of storms, they drew their boat up on land for the night.

Now one of the rustics, wanting a rope for suspending the stone for crushing the trodden grapes, his old one having broken, sneaked down to the sea, and, finding no one on board, untied the rope that tied the ship and brought it home to serve his business. In the morning the young Methymnaeans started an inquiry for their rope, and when no one confessed the theft they complained of the breach of hospitality and sailed away. They coasted along for some thirty furlongs and landed at the countryside where Daphnis and Chloe lived, which seemed a suitable place for rabbit hunting. They had no rope to use as a hawser, and so they twisted long green vines to make a rope, with which they tied the stern of their ship to the shore. Then they loosed their dogs to sniff out the game and set their nets where paths showed. The dogs ran here and there, and their yelping frightened the goats, who left their mountain haunts and dashed down to the shore. Finding nothing edible on the beach, the more venturesome approached the ship and ate up that green vine by which it was moored.

Now a swell set in, the breeze from the hills blowing out to sea, and the wash of the waves lifted the untied boat and carried it out to sea. When the Methymnaeans became aware of what had happened some ran down to the sea and others began to collect the dogs. All were shouting, so that everyone in the neighboring fields could hear and come to their assistance. But it was no use; the wind freshened and the boat was carried out on the tide. It was no little property the party had lost, and so they searched out the keeper of the goats, and when they found Daphnis they beat him and stripped him. One of them took a dog leash and bent his arms behind his back to tie him up. Daphnis cried out when he was beaten, and shouted for the rustics, and first of all for Lamon and Dryas, to help him. Their farm labor had given the old men tough sinews, and they stubbornly took Daphnis' part. It was their position that a judicial inquiry into the events must be made. When the others joined in the same demand, they appointed the cowherd Philetas as arbiter. He was the eldest of those present and enjoyed a reputation for strict probity among the villagers. First the Methymnaeans pronounced their charge, speaking plainly and concisely, because of having a cowherd for judge: "We came to these fields desiring to hunt. Our ship we tied with a green vine and left it on the shore, and we ourselves went hunting with our dogs. In the meanwhile this fellow's goats came down to the sea, ate up the vine, and loosed the ship. You yourselves saw it carried out to sea, and what quantity of valuables, think you, did it have on board? So and so much clothing has been lost, so and so much money. With that quantity a man could buy all the fields in this vicinity. In recompense we think it just to carry off this evil goatherd, who chooses to pasture his goats on the sea like a sailor."

Such charges did the Methymnaeans allege. Daphnis was in a sad plight by reason of his beating, but when he saw that Chloe was present he rose above his pain and spoke as follows: "I

pasture my goats very well. No single villager has ever complained that a goat of mine has browsed on or crushed his grow-
ing vine. But these are wicked huntsmen and their dogs are
badly trained. They run about wildly and bark fiercely, and like
wolves chase my goats from the hills and the plain down to the
sea. But, say you, they devoured the vine; of course, for they
could find no grass or shrub or thyme on the beach. But, say
you, by wind and sea the ship was lost; that was the work of
the storm, not the goats. But it contained clothing and money:
who in his senses could believe that a ship carrying such valuables would have a vine for a hawser?'' Thereupon Daphnis burst
into tears, and moved all the rustics to compassion. Philetas, the
judge, swore by Pan and the Nymphs that Daphnis was not at
fault and neither were the goats; only the sea and the wind
could be accused, and they were under a different jurisdiction.
Philetas' remarks did not appease the Methymnaeans, who flew
into a rage and were again on the point of tying Daphnis up.
This in turn annoyed the villagers, who flew upon them like starlings and grackles; soon they delivered Daphnis, who was now
fighting in his own defense. Very quickly the villagers, striking
out with their cudgels, routed the Methymnaeans, and did not
desist from their pursuit until they had driven them over their
borders.

While their friends were in pursuit of the Methymnaeans,
Chloe led Daphnis gently by the hand to the Nymphs and there
bathed his face, which was smeared with blood that a blow had
drawn from his nose. Then she brought a piece of sour dough
and a slice of cheese from her scrip and gave him to eat. But
what most refreshed him was the honey-sweet kiss with which
her tender lips caressed him. So near did Daphnis come to
calamity. And the affair did not end even there. The Methymnaeans made their way to their own country with difficulty, road
plodders now instead of voyagers, and with bruises instead of
dainties. They summoned an assembly of their fellow citizens,
and, declaring themselves suppliants, besought them to avenge
their wrongs. No single item of truth did they tell, for they
would be made a laughing stock for having been trounced and
chased by a few shepherds. But they formally accused the

Mytilenaeans of having seized their boat and plundered their property in a regular war. Their wounds gave them credit among their countrymen, who thought it proper to avenge young men who belonged to their first families. They therefore voted war without quarter against the Mytilenaeans, and ordered their general to launch ten vessels for the purpose of ravaging the enemy's coast. Since winter was at hand they did not think it safe to entrust a larger fleet to the sea.

Straightway on the following morning the commander put out to sea, employing his soldiers as rowers, and coasted along the farm lands of Mytilene. Here he seized many sheep and much grain and wine, the vintage being just completed, and he also took not a few laborers who were still at work there. He made a descent, too, on the fields of Chloe and Daphnis, and in a rapid raid carried off whatever booty he encountered. Daphnis was not then tending his goats, but had gone up to the forest to cut green leaves, to have fodder for his kids during the winter. He saw the incursion from his higher position, and hid himself in the hollow trunk of a dead beech tree. But Chloe was with the flocks. She was pursued and fled to the Nymphs, where she implored the soldiers, for the goddesses' sake, to spare her charges and herself. But it was of no avail. The Methymnaeans merely made jokes about the statues, and drove off the flocks and her with them, as if she were a sheep or a goat, striking her with vines.

Their vessels now being filled with plunder of all sorts, the Methymnaeans decided to sail no further, but, in fear of the winter and of their enemies, they started their voyage homeward. And so they put about, but had to toil hard at their oars, for there was no wind. When quiet had fallen Daphnis went down to the plain where they were used to pasture, but he could see no goats or come upon any sheep, nor find Chloe. Everything seemed deserted, and he noticed the pipe with which Chloe was used to amuse herself lying where she had thrown it. Then he cried out and lamented pitifully, and ran to the beech tree where they used to sit, and then to the sea, if he could catch sight of her there, and then to the Nymphs, where she had taken refuge when she was dragged off. There he flung himself down on the ground, and heaped reproaches on the Nymphs as traitors: " 'Twas from you that Chloe was ravaged, and could you endure to look on patiently? She it was who wove garlands for you, she it was who poured you libations of new milk, hers is this pipe that hangs here as an offering. Never a single goat of mine did a wolf ravage, but now marauders have carried off the whole flock and my fellow, their shepherdess. My goats they will flay, the sheep they will butcher—and Chloe will be living in the city. With what face can I return to my father and my mother without my goats and without Chloe? I will be called slacker and deserter! I have nothing to tend. Here will I lie down and wait for either death or another enemy raid. Ah, my Chloe, are these your feelings too? Do you remember this plain and these Nymphs and me? Or are you comforted by having the sheep and the goats as your companions in captivity?"

As Daphnis was thus lamenting, sunk in tears and sorrow, a profound sleep overtook him. Three Nymphs seemed to stand over him, tall and handsome women, half nude and barefoot, with loose-flowing hair, very like the statues. At first they seemed to express compassion for Daphnis, and then the eldest infused strength into him, saying, "Do not reproach us, Daphnis. Our care for Chloe is greater than yours. Even when she was an infant we took pity upon her, and when she lay in this cave we provided for her nurture. She has naught to do with pastures and Lamon's sheep. Now, too, her safety has been provided for; she will never be carried to Methymna as a slave, and will not be reckoned part of the enemy's spoil. Yonder Pan, whose statue stands beneath that pine tree, whom you have never honored with so much as a posy—yonder Pan have we entreated to become Chloe's champion. He is more accustomed to military matters than we, and frequently has he left his rustic abode to join in the din of battle. He will prove no easy enemy to the Methymnaeans. Do not then torment yourself, but rise up and show yourself to Lamon and Myrtale, who have sunk to the ground in their despair, thinking that you too are part of the plunder. Tomorrow Chloe will return to you with your goats and her sheep. Together you will pasture your flocks, and you will blow your pipes together. Afterwards Eros shall have charge of you."

When Daphnis had heard and seen these things he sprang up from his sleep, and filled with tears of both joy and sorrow, he did obeisance to the statues of the Nymphs and vowed to sacrifice the best of his she-goats if Chloe were saved. Then he ran to the pine tree where the statue of Pan stood—goat-limbed, horned, holding a pipe in one hand and a bucking goat in the other—and to him, too, he did obeisance, and offered prayer on behalf of Chloe, and vowed to sacrifice a he-goat. With difficulty did he bring his tears and prayers to an end at sunset; then, taking up the leaves which he had cut, he returned to his steading. His coming dispelled the grief of Lamon and his wife and filled them with joy, and then he took some food and went off to sleep—but not without tears. He prayed that he might again see the Nymphs in a dream, and he prayed that day would quickly come, for they had promised to restore Chloe on the morrow. Of all nights that appeared the longest. During that night, indeed, the following events transpired.

When the Methymnaean commander had sailed some ten furlongs he wished to refresh his soldiers, who were wearied by their exertions. He chose a promontory which projected into the sea in the shape of an extended crescent, within which the sea afforded a calmer haven than a regular port. Here he let his fleet ride at anchor, so that the rustics on shore should do it no mischief, and he released his men to indulge in peaceful pleasures. Their raids had provided them with a great plenty, and so they drank and frolicked and celebrated a kind of victory festival. The day was ended and night had put an end to their jollity, when suddenly the whole earth seemed to blaze out in bright flame, and the rhythmic beat of oars, as of a great fleet sailing toward them, was heard. Someone shouted to the commander to arm himself, one called out to another, some thought they were wounded, some lay in the likeness of death. It was all like a night battle, with no enemy there. After so terrifying a night the day following was more frightful still. The goats of Daphnis, and the she-goats, too, had branches filled with ivy berries on their horns, and the rams and ewes of Chloe howled like wolves. Chloe herself appeared, crowned with pine. The sea itself showed incredible prodigies. The anchors stuck fast in the bottom of the sea when men tried to raise them, and the oars were shattered when they dipped them into the water. Dolphins sprang out of the brine and struck the vessels with their tails and loosed their joints. From the top of the cliff which towered sheer over the headland there was heard the sound of a pipe, producing, however, not the pleasant notes a pipe yields, but terrifying hearers with a trumpet blast. The men were confounded, and ran to their weapons, and called out, "The enemy!" though they saw none. They prayed for night to return, to give them a truce to their terrors. To all who could think reasonably it was obvious that all that had transpired, the appearances and the sounds, were the work of Pan, who had some cause for anger against the sailors. But the cause they could not conjecture, for they had ravaged no sanctuary of Pan. About midday the general fell into a sleep, not without divine agency, and Pan himself appeared to him, and said:

"Men most impious and wicked of all, how did you dare perpetrate such mad outrages? The fields which are dear to me you have filled with the tumults of war. The herds of cows and goats and sheep which were my peculiar care you have taken as plunder. You have dragged from the altars a maiden of whom Eros wishes to fashion a tale of love. You showed no reverence for the Nymphs who were looking on, nor for me, Pan. Never, sailing with such booty as this, will you see Methymna again, never will you escape the terrors of the pipe which has confounded you. I will drown you in the sea and make you food for fish unless you restore to the Nymphs Chloe and Chloe's flock, both the goats and the sheep. Bestir yourselves, therefore, and disembark the girl and the animals. Then shall I be your guide by sea and hers by land.".

Bryaxis (for so was the commander called) was in great consternation. He sprang up and summoned the captains of the ships and ordered them to make an immediate search for Chloe among the captives. They found her quickly, for she was still crowned with pine where she sat, and brought her to the commander's presence as they found her. Her appearance he regarded as confirmation of his dream, and so brought her to land in the commander's own galley. No sooner had she stepped ashore than the sound of the pipe was again heard from the rock, not now warlike and terrifying, however, but with a shepherd's note, as when the flocks are brought out to pasture. The sheep, too, ran down the gangplank, without their horny hoofs slipping; the goats scampered down more boldly, for they were used to rough and steep going.

Now did all these creatures stand about Chloe in a circle like a chorus, skipping and bleating and otherwise manifesting their joy. The goats and sheep and cattle belonging to other shepherds remained in their place in the hold of the ship, as if they understood that it was not them the melody was calling. While everyone was struck with astonishment at these marvels and glorifying the power of Pan, marvels even more astonishing were taking place on both sea and land. Even before the Methymnaeans weighed their anchors the ships began to sail, and a dolphin leaping up out of the brine led the commander's ship on its way. On the other hand, Chloe's goats and sheep were led by the most ravishing music of the pipe, and none could see the piper. Sheep and goats moved forward, grazing as they went, entranced by the melody.

It was the time of the second feeding, when Daphnis, watching from a high rock, espied the flocks and Chloe. He shouted out, "O Nymphs and Pan!" and ran down to the plain. He twined his arms about Chloe, and fell fainting to the ground. With difficulty was he restored to his senses by Chloe's loving caresses and soothing embraces, and then made his way to their accustomed beech tree. Sitting under its trunk, he inquired how Chloe had managed to escape so many enemies, and she recounted the details—the ivy on the goats, the wolf howls of the sheep, the pine burgeoning on her head, the fire on the land, the beat of the oars in the sea, the diverse notes, warlike and peaceful, of the pipe, the terrifying night, and finally how, though she did not know the way, music guided her to her path. Daphnis recognized the dream sent by the Nymphs and the doings of Pan, and himself recounted all that he had seen and heard, and how, when he was going to die, he recovered life through the Nymphs. He then sent Chloe to fetch Dryas and Lamon and their wives and bring what was needful for sacrifice. In the meanwhile he himself took the choicest of the she-goats and crowned it with ivy, just as it had appeared to the enemy, and he poured over its horns a libation of milk, and sacrificed it to the Nymphs. Then he hung it up and flayed it, and deposited its hide as a votive offering.

When Chloe and those with her arrived he kindled a fire and boiled some of the meat and roasted some; the first portions he offered to the Nymphs and made libation to them with a bowl of new wine. Then he strewed leaves to form couches, where he gave himself to food and drink and gaiety; at the same time he kept his eye on the flocks so that no wolf should attack and complete the marauders' work. They also sang to the Nymphs certain old songs which had been composed by shepherds of an elder day. That night they slept in the field, and on the following day they took thought for Pan. The master goat of the flock they crowned with pine, and led him to the pine tree. Then when they had poured a libation and glorified the god, they slaughtered him, hung him, and flayed him. The flesh they boiled and roasted and laid out on leaves in the nearby meadow. The skin with its horns they fixed on the pine tree by the statue, a rustic offering to a rustic deity. They made offering also of the first portions of the flesh, and made libation from a larger bowl. Chloe sang and Daphnis piped. After these observances they reclined and turned to feasting. It chanced that Philetas came by, bringing little wreaths and clusters on vines with the leaves upon them as an offering to Pan. Philetas was followed by the youngest of his sons, Tityros, a ruddy-haired, hazel-eyed lad, fair of complexion and high-spirited. He came bounding lightly along, skipping like a kid. All sprang up then, and joined in crowning Pan and in hanging the vine from the foliage of the pine tree. Then they made the newcomers recline by them and join in their revel. Then, as old men do when they are a little softened with drink, they told one another many tales of their shepherd adventures when they were young, and of how many pirate forays they had survived. One boasted of having killed a wolf, another that he was second only to Pan in piping. This last was the vaunt of Philetas.

Daphnis and Chloe pressed him most urgently to share his art with them and to play his pipe for the festivity to the god whose delight was the pipe. Philetas complained that old age had made his breath short, but he consented nevertheless, and took Daphnis' pipe. But 'twas too small a pipe for so high an art, suited only for being blown upon by the lips of a boy, so he sent Tityros to fetch his own pipe from his cottage, which was ten furlongs away. Tityros threw off his jacket and dashed off at a run, like a fawn. Lamon meanwhile promised to regale them with the story of Syrinx (the "Pipe"), which a Sicilian shepherd had chanted to him for the fee of a goat and a pipe.

"Syrinx, you must know, was of old not an instrument, but a beautiful maiden with a melodious voice. She fed her goats, sported with the Nymphs, and sang as she now does. As she was thus pasturing, sporting, and singing, Pan approached her and sought to persuade her to yield to his desires, promising that all her she-goats would bear twins at a birth. The girl mocked at his suit, saying she would never accept a lover who was neither goat nor wholly human. Pan darted after her to take her perforce, and Syrinx fled Pan and his violence. When she was wearied in her flight she hid in some reeds and so disappeared in a marsh. In his rage Pan slashed down the reeds, and when he could not find the girl and perceived what had happened, he contrived this instrument. The reeds which he bound with wax he made unequal, because their love had been unequal. And so she who was once a beautiful maiden is now a musical pipe."

Lamon had just finished recounting his legend and Philetas was thanking him for telling a story that was sweeter than any song, when Tityros arrived bringing his father's pipe. This was a large instrument made of good-sized reeds and ornamented with brass over the junctures of wax. One might suppose that this was the very instrument which Pan first fashioned. Philetas then arose, sat himself upright in a chair, and tried the pipe to see whether its passages were clear; and when he found that his breath passed through with no hindrance, he blew upon it with such great power and variety that the hearer might suppose he was listening to a symphony of flutes. Gradually he moderated his force and changed to a sweeter strain. He exhibited all the art of pastoral music, piping a melody appropriate for a herd of cows, another suitable for goats, a third agreeable to sheep.

The sheep's note was sweet, the cattle's loud, the goats' shrill; in a word, that one pipe simulated many pipes.

The others lay about, listening in silent delight, but Dryas arose and bade Philetas play the Dionysiac strain, and himself performed the vintage dance. First he represented a man plucking clusters, then one carrying baskets of grapes, and then one treading the vine, and then one filling the tuns, and then one tasting the must. All these figures Dryas danced with such grace and precision that the onlookers imagined they beheld the vines and the press and the casks and Dryas actually drinking.

Thus the third old man also won acclaim, by his dancing, and this moved Chloe and Daphnis to bestir themselves. They arose briskly, and danced out Lamon's story. Daphnis imitated Pan, and Chloe Syrinx. He urged and begged, and she smiled scornfully; he pursued, running on tiptoe in imitation of hoofs, and she simulated a maiden exhausted by flight. Then Chloe hid herself in the woods, as a substitute for the marsh, and Daphnis took Philetas' large pipe and played upon it first a mournful strain, like a lover's, then a lovesick strain, as of a pleader, then a summoning strain, as of one on a search. Philetas marveled at the performance; he sprang up and kissed Daphnis and made him a present of the pipe, praying that he would find so worthy a successor to leave it to.

Daphnis dedicated his own little pipe to Pan, then he kissed Chloe as if he had truly found her after losing her, and then drove his flock off, piping as he went. Night coming on, Chloe took her flock home also, guiding them by the tune of her pipe. And so the goats kept close by the sheep, and Daphnis walked close by Chloe. Thus until nightfall they kept close by one another, and they agreed to drive their flocks out earlier the following morning, and so in fact they did. As soon as day dawned they went out to pasture, and when they had offered salutations first to the Nymphs and then to Pan they sat themselves down under the oak tree and piped. There they kissed each other and embraced each other and lay on the ground side by side, but did nothing further. Then they arose and attended to their food; their drink was wine mixed with milk.

These pastimes rendered them warmer and bolder. They vied

with each other in amorous contests, and after a little advanced to pledging one another with oaths. Daphnis swore by Pan, at whose pine he took his oath, that he would not live without Chloe, not even for the space of a single day. And Chloe swore to Daphnis by the Nymphs, to whose grotto she went for her oath, that she would always love Daphnis, in life and in death. So great was Chloe's simplicity, she being but a girl, that when she emerged from the grotto she required Daphnis to swear a second oath. "For," she said, "Pan himself is a lover, and yet unfaithful; he was in love with Pitys and in love with Syrinx, and yet he never stops pestering the Dryads and annoying the Epimelian Nymphs. One who is so careless of his own pledges will be careless of punishing you, even if you should have more mistresses than there are reeds in this pipe. Swear to me then by this herd of goats and by that she-goat who nurtured you that you will never desert Chloe as long as she remains faithful to you. But if she wrongs you and the Nymphs, avoid her, hate her, kill her as you would a wolf." Daphnis was delighted at her expression of distrust, and so, taking his stand in the midst of his herd, and grasping a he-goat in one hand and a she-goat in the other, he swore that he would love Chloe, who loved him, and that if she ever preferred another to Daphnis he would kill himself instead of her. She was much pleased and she believed him, as was natural for a girl and for one who thought that goats and sheep were the proper deities for shepherds and goat-herds.

3 *When the people of Mytilene learned of the hostile* descent of the ten ships and were moreover informed, by some who came from the region affected, of the plunder that had been taken, they thought the action of the Methymnaeans was not to be endured, and determined to move a force against them forthwith. They mustered three thousand infantry and five hundred cavalry under the general Hippasos, and because the sea was unsafe during the winter, they dispatched them by land.

Hippasos marched forth, but neither devastated the Methym-naean countryside nor plundered its herds or other property of farmers and shepherds, thinking such more befitting marauders than a general. Rather did he march directly to the city itself, to fall upon it while the gates were unguarded. When he was still about a hundred furlongs distant a herald carrying terms of truce met him. The Methymnaeans had now discovered from their captives that the Mytilenaeans themselves had no knowl-edge of the provocatory incident, and that the insolent behavior of the young men had drawn upon them the vengeance of farm-ers and shepherds. They therefore repented of making war against a neighboring city with precipitateness rather than pru-dence, and were eager to restore all their plunder and resume peaceful intercourse by land and sea. Although Hippasos had been elected commander in chief with full powers, he neverthe-less sent the herald on to Mytilene, and himself pitched camp about ten furlongs from Methymna, to await orders from his home city. After an interval of two days a messenger arrived with orders for him to receive the restored booty, to refrain from any act of hostility, and to march home again. When it came to a choice between war and peace, the city found peace preferable.

So was settled that war between the Methymnaeans and Mytilenaeans, the beginning and end of which were equally un-expected. But more formidable than war was the winter which followed for Daphnis and Chloe. A sudden and heavy fall of snow blocked off all the roads and shut the farmers indoors. Wintry torrents rushed down the hills, ice froze hard, the trees seemed overwhelmed with their weight of snow, and all land disappeared except a little at fountains and streams. No one took flocks out of doors. At cockcrow they would build up a big fire, and some twisted linen, some wove goat's-hair, and some fashioned nets for birds. At the same time they took care to supply the mangers of the cattle with chaff, the cotes of the goats and sheep with leaves, and the sties of the pigs with holmberries and acorns.

When everyone was thus of necessity housebound, the farmers and shepherds generally were pleased at this respite from their labors, this opportunity to take leisurely meals, and to sleep long hours; to them winter appeared a more agreeable season than summer or autumn or even spring. But Chloe and Daphnis could only think of their interrupted delights—their kisses, their embraces, their happy meals together. They passed nights of sleeplessness and sorrow, and awaited the return of spring as a new birth after death. They were stung with pain if a scrip out of which they had eaten came into their hands, or if they chanced to see a pail from which they had drunk together, or a pipe, now cast away in neglect, which had once been a lover's gift. They prayed to the Nymphs and Pan to release them from these woes and again to show them and their flocks the sunshine; and as they prayed they sought some device by which they might see one another. Chloe was altogether at a loss and helpless, for her foster mother was always at her side, teaching her to card wool and whirl the spindle and speaking also of matrimony. But Daphnis had more leisure and was more inventive than the girl, and so contrived the following device for seeing Chloe.

In front of Dryas' cottage, and indeed under the cottage itself, there grew two large myrtles and an ivy. The myrtles were near each other, and the ivy between them extended its shoots on either side like a vine, and by intermingling its leaves with theirs formed a grotto-like arbor. From the vines hung abundant berries, as large as grapes. Quantities of winter birds flocked to the place for want of food elsewhere; there were blackbirds, thrushes, wood pigeons, starlings, and other birds that feed on ivy berries. On the pretext of hunting these birds Daphnis filled his scrip with honeyed cakes and went out; to obviate all suspicion he took birdlime and snares also. Though the distance was not more than ten furlongs, the snow was still solid and made the road toilsome; but neither fire nor water nor Scythian snow can stand in the way of love.

On the run, then, Daphnis arrived at Dryas' cottage, and after shaking the snow off his legs he set his snares, smeared long sticks with birdlime, and sat down to fret over the birds and Chloe. As for the birds, quantities came and a large number were caught, so that Daphnis was fully occupied in collecting them, killing them, and plucking their feathers. But no one at all came out of the cottage, man, woman, or chicken; the whole household were hugging the fire inside. Daphnis was completely at a loss, and thought he had come at an "ill-birded" time. He ventured to look about for an excuse for knocking on the door, and pondered on what he could plausibly say. "I have come to get fire for kindling." . . . "But you have neighbors within a furlong." . . . "I came to ask for bread." . . . "But your scrip is stuffed with victuals." . . . "Please give me wine." . . . "But you had your vintage only the other day." . . . "A wolf has chased me." . . . "But where are the wolf's tracks?" . . . "I have come to hunt birds." . . . "Well, then, you have hunted; why don't you go home?" . . . "I want to see Chloe." . . . "But who could make such a profession to a girl's father and mother? Everywhere I am balked into silence; nothing I can say is free of suspicion. It is better to hold my peace. Chloe I shall see in the spring, since I am fated, as it seems, not to see her during the winter." Such was the course of his reverie, and so he gathered his bag together, and prepared to leave. But, as if Eros took pity upon him, the following then transpired.

Dryas and his household had sat down to table. The meat was portioned out, the bread was served, and the wine bowl mixed. One of the sheep dogs snatched some meat while no one was watching and ran outdoors. Dryas was annoyed (it was his portion the dog had taken), and so he grabbed a stick and followed the dog's tracks like another dog. His chase took him by the ivy arbor, where he spied Daphnis slinging his catch over his shoulders, determined to leave. Meat and dog alike immediately left Dryas' mind, and he shouted, "Hello there, boy!" He embraced him and kissed him and took him by the hand and brought him into the house. When the lovers saw each other they nearly collapsed, but they found strength to stand upright while they saluted and kissed one another; in point of fact their embrace served as a buttress to keep them from falling.

Beyond his expectations, then, Daphnis got a kiss and Chloe herself. He sat down near the fire, and from his shoulders he unloaded onto the table the wood pigeons and the thrushes, and he explained how he had found keeping at home tedious and gone ahunting, and how he had caught the birds who were greedy for the myrtles and ivy, some with snares and some with birdlime. The family praised his energy, and bade him eat— what the dog had left—and told Chloe to pour him a drink. She was very willing, but served the others first, and Daphnis after them. She pretended to be angry because, having come so far, he was going to run away without seeing her. Nevertheless, before she handed him his drink she sipped a little of it and then gave it to him. And he, though he was thirsty, drank very slowly, making his pleasure as long as possible by his delay.

The table was quickly cleared of bread and meat. Then as they sat about they inquired for Myrtale and Lamon, and they felicitated them on their good fortune in having such a provider for their old age. Daphnis was very pleased at being so commended in the hearing of Chloe. And when they insisted that he stay on the ground that they were going to sacrifice to Dionysos on the following day, it wanted but little for Daphnis to adore them instead of the god. He immediately produced the store of honeyed cakes from his scrip and the birds he had caught, and then they prepared for their evening meal. A second mixing bowl was set out, and a second fire was lighted. And when night was fallen they regaled themselves with a second repast, and afterwards they told stories and sang songs, and so went to bed, Chloe with her mother, and Dryas with Daphnis. Chloe had no profit of this arrangement except that on the following day she would see Daphnis. Daphnis did enjoy a hollow kind of delight; he thought it was pleasurable to sleep even with Chloe's father, and he frequently embraced him and kissed him, dreaming that he was doing so to Chloe.

When day dawned the cold was very sharp, and the blast of the north wind parched everything. Dryas and his household arose, sacrificed a year-old ram to Dionysos, and kindled a big fire to cook the dinner. While Nape was baking bread and Dryas boiling the ram, Daphnis and Chloe were free to go to the arbor where the ivy was, and again they set snares and smeared birdlime and caught a good quantity of birds. They also enjoyed constant kisses and delightful conversation. " 'Twas for you I came, Chloe." "I know, Daphnis." " 'Tis because of you I destroy these poor blackbirds. What do I mean to you? Do you think of me." "I do think of you, by the Nymphs by whom I swore in that grotto: we shall go there again when the snow has melted." "But there is so much of it, Chloe, I'm afraid I shall melt before it does." "Courage, Daphnis, the sun is warm." "Would it were as warm as the fire that burns my heart." "You are joking, to deceive me." "No, by the goats by whom you bade me swear." Thus antiphonally did Chloe respond to Daphnis, like an echo. When Nape called them into the house they ran in, bringing a more plentiful bag than on the day before. And when they had poured the first libation to Dionysos, they crowned their heads with ivy and sat down to eat. And when the time was come, they shouted Iacchus! and Evoe! and sent Daphnis on his way, filling his scrip with bread and meat. They also gave him the wood pigeons and thrushes to take to Lamon and Myrtale, for they themselves could catch others as long as the snow lasted and the ivy berries did not fail. And so he departed, kissing them all before Chloe, so that her kiss might remain with him unalloyed. Many other times did he make the trip, on other pretexts, so that their winter proved not altogether devoid of love.

And now was spring beginning; the snow melted, the earth reappeared, grass was sprouting. The other shepherds drove their flocks to pasture, but ahead of them all were Chloe and Daphnis, for they were themselves in the service of a greater shepherd. First of all they hastened to the Nymphs and the grotto, thence to Pan and the pine, then to the oak tree, under which they sat, pasturing their flocks and kissing one another. They searched for flowers also, wishing to crown the deities. These the nourishing zephyrs and the warming sun had but newly caused to shoot; but they did find violets and narcissus and pimpernel and others that the early spring brings forth. Chloe and Daphnis also tasted the new milk of goats and ewes, and they wreathed the statues and made libation to them. Then they drew the first notes from their pipes, as if challenging the nightingales to sing, and these answered softly from the thickets, and after a little they gave a precise rendition of Itys, as if recalling the song after a long silence. Here was heard the bleating of the flock, and then lambs were frisking or stooping under their mothers and drawing at the teat. Those that had never lambed were pursued by rams, who leaped upon those they caught, serving one after another. There were similar chases among the goats and more passionate leaps upon the she-goats, and among the bucks there were fights over their females; each goat possessed his own, and kept guard lest a surreptitious adulterer approach them. Such spectacles as these might have aroused even aged spectators to the stirrings of love: Daphnis and Chloe, who were young and bursting with vigor and who had now for a long while been seeking the path to love, were set afire by these sounds and melted by these sights, and they too, but especially Daphnis, sought for something beyond kisses and embraces. Having been kept housebound and idle during the winter, his youthful vigor was running over; he was impetuous in his kisses and passionate in his embraces and more curious and bolder in all the works of love.

He begged Chloe to grant him his full desires and to lie side by side with him flesh to flesh for a longer space than they were used to do, for this alone was wanting of those precepts taught by Philetas as the sole remedy to assuage the pangs of love. She inquired what there could be more than kisses and embraces and lying by one another, and what it was he was resolved to do when he was naked and lying by her naked. "The same," he said, "as the rams do to the sheep, and the goats to the she-goats. You see how, after they have performed their deed, the shes no longer flee the hes, nor do the hes weary themselves with pursuit, but for the future they graze together, as if they enjoyed mutual pleasure. The act, it seems, must be sweet indeed, and it vanquishes the sting of love." "But do you not see, Daphnis," said Chloe, "in the case of the she-goats and he-goats, the ewes and the rams, that the males take their active part in an upright position and the females their passive part similarly in an upright position, the ones leaping upon the others, who receive them upon their backs? But you think I should lie down with you, and at that naked—but those animals are much shaggier than I am when I am undressed." Daphnis agreed to her arguments. He lay by her for a long while, but not understanding how to gratify his eager passion, he raised her up and in imitation of the goats clung fast to her from behind. But then, being still more at a loss, he sat down and wept at the thought that he was stupider than a ram in the works of love.

Daphnis had a certain neighbor who farmed his own land, Chromis by name, whose body had now passed its prime. This Chromis had a wife who came from the city; she was young and pretty and more graceful than countrywomen, and her name was Lycainion. Every day this Lycainion watched Daphnis driving his goats by, in the morning out to pasture and in the evening back home again, and she conceived a desire to get him for her lover by ensnaring him with gifts. One time she waylaid him when he was alone and gave him a pipe and honey in the comb and a scrip of deerskin. She was afraid to speak out, because she divined that he was in love with Chloe, for she saw him always sticking to the girl's company. Previously she had conjectured their love only from their nods and smiles; but early on the morning of this day she pretended to Chromis that she was going to help a neighbor who was in childbed, and followed after Daphnis and Chloe. From behind some bushes where she could not be seen she heard all that they said and saw all that they did, and even observed Daphnis' weeping. She was sorry for the young things, and thought she could do two good deeds at once—help them out of their trouble and ease her own desire. This was her scheme.

On the following day, using that same woman in childbed as an excuse, she went openly to the oak tree where Daphnis and Chloe sat and came up to them with a fine imitation of a woman in a panic. "Save me, Daphnis," said she; "save an unhappy woman. Of my twenty geese an eagle has carried off the best. Then he couldn't lift it high enough to carry it to yonder rock, where he has his eyrie, and has fallen down with it in this very wood. In the name of the Nymphs and yonder Pan, do you come into that wood with me, for I am afraid to go alone, and save my goose for me; do not let my even score of geese be spoiled. Perhaps you can kill the eagle and then he will not carry off your many lambs and kids. Chloe will watch your flock in the meantime; surely the goats know her, for she always pastures close by you."

Daphnis had no suspicion of what was to come, so he arose and, crook in hand, followed after Lycainion. She led him as far as possible from Chloe, and when they were in a very thick wood she made him sit down by a spring. "Daphnis," said she, "you are in love with Chloe; this I learned last night from the Nymphs. In a dream they showed me the tears you shed yesterday and bade me save you by teaching you that love is more than kisses and embraces and such things as rams and goats do. There are leaps, indeed, but far sweeter than those, for their pleasure is longer. If then you would be delivered from your pains and find the delights you crave, come, be my apprentice, and I, in gracious obedience to the Nymphs, will teach you your lessons." Daphnis could hardly restrain himself for pleasure, but like the rustic and goatherd and lover and callow youth that he was, he fell at Lycainion's feet and implored her to teach him as quickly as possible that art of love so that he might have his desire with Chloe. Moreover, as if he were going to learn some mystery great and heaven-sent, he promised to give Lycainion a suckling kid and soft cheeses made of the first milk and the she-goat with them. When Lycainion discovered such ingenuousness as she had never expected of a goatherd she began to tutor Daphnis after this fashion. She bade him sit down by her directly and to bestow kisses upon her, of the customary quality and quantity, and in the midst of his kissing to embrace her and lie down on the ground. When he had sat down and kissed her and lain down, and she discovered that he was now able to act and was bursting with swollen energy, she raised him from his reclining position to his side and featly placed herself underneath, and then put him in the way of the desired path. Nature provided instruction on what was next to be done.

When this lesson in love was consummated Daphnis, as innocent as before, was eager to run to Chloe and immediately put into practice the lesson he had learned, as if afraid that he would forget it if he delayed. But Lycainion held him back and said. "There is something else you must learn, Daphnis. I happen to be a mature woman, and so you have not hurt me. Long ago another man educated me, and received my maidenhood for his tuition. But when Chloe grapples with you in this wrestling match she will cry out and weep and bleed as if she were wounded. Yet you must not shrink from the blood. When you have persuaded her to yield to you take her to this spot where even if she cries out no one will hear, and even if she weeps no one will see, and even if she bleeds she can wash herself in this spring. And remember that it was I who made a man of you for Chloe." When Lycainion had imparted her instructions she went off to another part of the woods, as if still in search of her goose. But Daphnis reflected upon what she had said and abated his former impetuosity. He hesitated to trouble Chloe more than by kissing and embracing, nor did he wish her to cry out as against an enemy, nor to weep as one in anguish, nor to bleed as one wounded. Being but a novice, he dreaded blood and thought that only a wound could produce gore. He therefore resolved to take only the customary pleasures with Chloe, and emerged from the wood. He went to where she was sitting, and found her winding a chaplet of violets. He told a story about saving the goose from the talons of the eagle, and then embraced her close and kissed her, as he had kissed Lycainion in that pleasurable exchange: so much, at least, was free of danger. She then fitted the chaplet on to his head, and kissed his hair as being better than violets. Then from her scrip she produced a cake of figs and slices of bread, and gave him to eat. And while he was eating she snatched morsels from his mouth, and so ate like a fledgling bird.

While they were eating, and taking more kisses than victuals, a fishing boat was seen coasting by. There was no wind, but a dead calm, and hence need of rowing, and the crew rowed briskly. They were hurrying in order to bring fresh to the city, for a certain rich man there, some fish they had newly caught among the rocks. As sailors are wont to do to beguile their weariness, those sailors did as they raised their oars. One of them, the boatswain, raised a sea chantey, and the rest, like a chorus, shouted out in unison at intervals, following the rhythm of his voice. When they did this in the wide-open sea the sound disappeared, for the voices were dispersed over a great stretch of air. But when they ran under a headland and entered a hollow and crescent-shaped bay, a loud sound came to shore, and the boatswain's chants were distinctly heard. Here a deep valley sloped down from the plain above, received the sound into itself like a musical instrument, and returned a precise imitation of every note it received, the sound of the oars being quite distinct from the voices of the sailors. The effect was pleasing to the listener. The sound of the sea came first, and that from the land continued as much longer as it was later in beginning. Daphnis understood the process, and paid attention only to the sea. He took pleasure watching the ship disappear in the distance like a bird in the air, and he tried to retain some of the chanteys to adapt the tunes to his pipe. But for Chloe this was the first experience of what is called the echo. She looked now toward the sea, where the sailors were singing their responses, and now she turned to the land, looking for the source of the antiphonal chant. When they had sailed by and there was silence even in the valley she asked Daphnis whether there was another sea back of the headland with another ship sailing in it and other sailors who sang the same songs and then fell silent at the same time. Daphnis smiled upon her sweetly and gave her a kiss still sweeter, and then he put the wreath of violets upon her head and began to tell her the legend of Echo, asking ten more kisses as reward for teaching her the tale.

"Of Nymphs, my girl, there are many kinds—Meliae or Ash Nymphs, Dryads or Oak Nymphs, and Eleiai or Marsh Nymphs. All are beautiful, and all are musical. The daughter of one of these Nymphs was Echo; she was mortal, for her father was a mortal, but she was beautiful, for her mother was beautiful. She was nurtured by the Nymphs and was taught by the Muses to play the pipe, the flute, the lyre, the harp, and all the art of music. And so when the maiden reached her bloom she danced along with the Nymphs and sang along with the Muses. She avoided all males, whether human or divine, for she loved maidenhood. But Pan was angry with the girl; he was jealous of her music and unsuccessful in suing for her beauty, and so he visited such madness upon shepherds and goatherds that like dogs or wolves they tore her limb from limb and scattered her members, still uttering song, over all the land. All the members Earth hid away as a favor to the Nymphs. But her music Earth preserved, and by the will of the Muses she sends forth her voice and, as once she did when she was a girl, she imitates all things —gods, mortals, instruments, beasts; she even imitates the piping of Pan himself. When Pan hears this, he springs up and rushes over the mountains in pursuit, not to obtain satisfaction of his love but rather to find who his secret disciple might be." When Daphnis had finished his tale, Chloe gave him not merely ten kisses, but kissed him over and over again—and Echo reproduced almost the same sounds, as if to bear witness that Daphnis had not falsified.

Now the sun grew warmer each day, for the spring was drawing to a close and the summer beginning, and the new delights of the summer season again fell to their lot. Daphnis swam in the rivers, and Chloe bathed in the fountains. Daphnis played his pipe in rivalry with the pines and Chloe sang in competition with the nightingales. They chased chattering crickets, they caught chirping grasshoppers, they gathered flowers, or shook trees and ate their fruit. Sometimes they lay side by side naked, and a single goatskin covered them. Chloe would soon have become a woman if the matter of the blood had not terrified Daphnis. Indeed, fearing lest passion should vanquish reason, often he would not allow Chloe to expose her nakedness. At this Chloe wondered, but she was ashamed to inquire the reason.

That summer saw a crowd of suitors for Chloe. Numbers came to Dryas from many places to ask for Chloe in marriage. Some brought gifts, others made many large promises. Nape was elated with her hopes, and advised that Chloe be married off: a girl of such an age should no longer be kept at home, or very likely she would soon lose her maidenhood while pasturing and make a man of some shepherd in return for apples or flowers. The best course (said Nape) was to make a housewife of Chloe, and themselves accept the numerous presents and keep them for their own legitimate son; not long before a boy had been born to them. Dryas was sometimes mollified by these arguments, for the gifts which the several suitors enumerated were beyond what a shepherd girl might expect; but sometimes he reflected that the girl was superior to her rustic suitors and that if she should ever find her true parents she would make him very rich. And so he put his decision off, dragging the answer out from one time to the next, and in the meanwhile he profited by the suitors' gifts. When Chloe learned of all this she was deeply grieved, but for a long while she kept it secret from Daphnis because she did not wish to cause him pain. But when he urged her and persisted in his inquiries and seemed more distressed at not knowing than he would be knowing, she told him the whole story—about the suitors, numerous and wealthy; about Nape's eagerness for her marriage and the arguments she used; about Dryas' refusal to say her nay and his postponement of his decision until the vintage.

Upon this Daphnis was beside himself. He sat down and wept bitterly, and declared that if Chloe was no more a shepherdess he would die—and not alone he, but all the sheep too when they lost such a mistress. Then he collected himself and took heart, and he resolved to persuade Chloe's father and enroll himself as one of the suitors, and he hoped that he would prevail over the others. One thing troubled him: Lamon was not rich, and this alone made Daphnis' hope a slender thing. Nevertheless, he resolved to declare himself a suitor, and Chloe agreed with this resolution. He did not have sufficient boldness to speak to Lamon, but he did venture to hint of his love to Myrtale and to adduce arguments in favor of his marriage. At night Myrtale communicated the matter to Lamon. Lamon received her intercession very harshly, and rebuked her sharply for wishing to marry a shepherd's daughter to a lad whose infant tokens promised a high fortune and who, if he found his own kindred, would make them free and the owners of broad fields. Because of Daphnis' great love Myrtale feared that if he were made to despair of the marriage altogether he might venture on some fatal step, and so she reported different grounds for Lamon's refusal: "We are poor, my boy, and so we require a bride who will bring us something by way of dowry; they, on the other hand, are rich, and demand rich suitors. But go and persuade Chloe, and have her persuade her father not to demand too much, and to marry her to you. I am sure that she loves you, and would rather sleep with a poor man who is handsome than with a monkey who is rich."

Myrtale never expected that Dryas would agree to the proposal, for he had much richer suitors, but she thought that she had neatly parried the question of marriage. Daphnis could find no defect in what she said, but was far short of obtaining his desires and so did what is customary for needy lovers: he wept and again invoked the aid of the Nymphs. At night as he slept the Nymphs did appear to him, in the same posture and dress as they had done before, and again the eldest spoke: "Chloe's marriage is in the charge of another deity, but we shall supply you with gifts which will appease Dryas. The ship of the Methymnaean gallants whose vine hawser your goats once devoured was that same day carried far out to sea by a wind, but at night when a gale from the deep churned the sea it was dashed against the rocky cliffs. The ship and its abundant freight were destroyed, but a purse containing three thousand drachmas was spewed up by the waves and lies hidden under seaweed near the cadaver of a dolphin. Hence no wayfarers approach, for the stench of the rotting carcass makes them hurry by. But do you approach, and when you have approached, take up, and when you have taken up, give. Enough for the present not to seem a beggar; in time you will be even rich."

Thus they said, and they departed along with the night. At break of day Daphnis sprang up overjoyed, and he drove his goats to pasture with exuberant haste. When he had kissed Chloe and bowed down to the Nymphs he went down to the sea, as if he wished to sluice himself, and he walked along the beach, near where the waves broke, seeking the three thousand drachmas. It wanted no tedious search, for the dolphin, cast up and rotting and emitting an evil smell, lay in his path; using the stench as his guide, he approached the spot, removed the seaweed, and found the purse full of silver. This he took up and put into his scrip, but he did not leave the spot before pronouncing blessings upon the Nymphs and upon the sea itself. Though a shepherd, he now thought the sea more agreeable than the land, for it had helped him win Chloe for wife.

Now that he had got possession of three thousand drachmas Daphnis thought himself the richest man in the world, not merely of the farmers of his countryside. Without delay he hurried to Chloe, recounting his dream, showed her the purse, bade her keep the flocks until he should return, and himself swaggered off to Dryas. He found him at his grain threshing with Nape and boldly broke into the subject of marriage: "Give me Chloe to wife. I know how to pipe well, to prune vines, and to plant slips. I know how to plow and winnow. My skill as a shepherd Chloe can bear witness to: fifty she-goats I received, and I have doubled their number. We used to send our she-goats out to stud, but I have raised fine, large bucks. I am young, and as your neighbor you know me to be of irreproachable character. Me a she-goat suckled, as a ewe did Chloe. Being to this degree superior to other suitors, I shall not be found inferior in the matter of gifts. They will offer goats and sheep and a yoke of mangy oxen and corn not fit even to feed roosters; but from me here you have three thousand drachmas. Only let no one know of this, not even Lamon my father." With these words he handed him the money and embraced and kissed him.

Dryas and Nape, seeing a sum of money larger than they ever expected to see, immediately engaged to give him Chloe, and promised to procure Lamon's consent also. Nape remained at the threshing floor with Daphnis, driving the cows around and threshing the grain with the drag. Dryas carefully deposited the purse where he had laid up Chloe's birth tokens, and then quickly betook himself to Lamon and Myrtale, on the novel errand of wooing for a husband. He found them measuring newly winnowed barley, and in very low spirits because the yield was almost less than the seeds they had planted. Dryas tried to console them by avowing that that was a common and widespread complaint that season, and then asked for Daphnis as a husband for Chloe. He said that others were making large offers; from them, however, he would take nothing, but rather himself give them something. The young people had been brought up together, and by pasturing together had joined in a mutual affection which could not easily be broken. Now they were of suitable age to consummate their marriage. Such arguments and more did Dryas use, holding three thousand drachmas at home as a contingent fee for his persuasiveness. Lamon could no longer plead poverty, for the other party made no scruple of

that, nor could he plead Daphnis' youth, for he was now verg-
ing on manhood. His true objection, that Daphnis was superior
to such a marriage, he could not utter; and so, after a long
silence, he answered as follows:

"It is very fair of you to favor your neighbors over strangers
and to refuse to count a rich man superior to an honorable poor
man. For this may Pan and the Nymphs love you. I myself am
also eager for this marriage. I should be mad if, being as old as I
am and in need of additional hands for my work, I should not
regard a connection with your house as a great advantage.
Chloe, too, is a most desirable match, for she is a beautiful girl
of excellent character and accomplishments. But I am only a
bound tenant and not really master of what is mine; it is therefore essential that my master be apprised of these things and
grant his consent. Come, then, let us put the marriage off to the
autumn. People from the city with whom I have spoken tell me
that he will come here at that time. Then shall they be man and
wife, but for the present let them love one another as brother
and sister. This, too, must I tell you, Dryas: the young man for
whom you are suing is superior to us all." So saying, he saluted
Dryas and handed him a drink, for it was now midday and very
hot, and then he escorted him part of his way home, showing
him every courtesy.

Lamon's last expression was not lost upon Dryas, and as he
walked he pondered in his mind who Daphnis might be: "He
was suckled by a she-goat, as if by the special providence of the
gods. He is very handsome, and bears no resemblance to that
flat-nosed old man and his bald-pated wife. He could dispose
of three thousand drachmas; no goatherd is likely to possess so
many pears. Did someone expose him as Chloe was exposed? Did
Lamon find him as I found her? Were there tokens left with
him like those I found? May it be so, Pan and ye dear Nymphs!
Perhaps when he finds his own people he will find something
of Chloe's secrets also." Such were his thoughts and such his
reveries until he reached his threshing floor. There he found
Daphnis in eager suspense for his tidings, and so he steadied
him by addressing him as son-in-law. He promised to celebrate

the marriage in the autumn and gave him his right hand in pledge that Chloe would belong to none other than Daphnis.

Quicker than thought, without stopping to eat or drink, Daphnis ran to Chloe. He found her milking and making cheese and gave her the glad tidings of the marriage. For the future he kissed her not surreptitiously but openly as his wife, and he shared her work. He drew milk into pails, fixed the cheeses on the racks, placed the lambs and kids under their dams. When their tasks were in order, they washed themselves, ate and drank, and went out in search of ripe fruit. It was the productive season, and there was a great plenty; there were many pears, wild and cultivated, and many apples. Some were already fallen to the ground, some still on their branches. Those on the ground had a better flavor, those on the branches a more blooming look; these had a bouquet as of wine, those shone like gold. One apple tree had been stripped and possessed neither fruit nor leaf, and all its branches were bare. One solitary apple hung at the top of the highest branch; it was large and beautiful and by itself surpassed the fragrance of a whole heap. The gatherer had feared to climb so high, or had neglected to pluck it; perhaps he saved the beautiful apple for a lovesick shepherd. When Daphnis saw that apple he was eager to climb up and pluck it, and paid no heed to Chloe when she sought to prevent him. Being thus unheeded, she strode off and followed her flock. But Daphnis scaled the tree to the point where he could reach the apple, and he brought it as a gift to Chloe, and uttered the following speech to the angry girl: "Maiden, this apple the beauteous Hours planted, and a noble tree nurtured; the sun ripened it, and Fortune watched over it. Having eyes to see, I could not leave it behind where it would fall to the ground, where a grazing sheep might tread upon it, or a creeping serpent void his slime upon it, or time consume it where it lay —especially when it had been admired and praised. An apple did Aphrodite receive as the prize for her beauty; an apple do I give to you as the palm of victory. You both have like arbiters of your beauty, for Paris was a shepherd, as I am a goatherd." So saying, he placed the apple in Chloe's bosom, and she, as he drew near, kissed him. So Daphnis did not repent his boldness in climbing to such a height, for he received a kiss more precious than an apple of gold.

4 There came a man from Mytilene, a fellow serf of Lamon's, and told him that a little before the vintage their master would come to discover whether the incursion of the Methymnaeans had worked any injury to his fields. The summer was already waning and autumn approaching, so Lamon worked to give everything an agreeable appearance for his master's sojourn. He purged the springs so that he might have pure water; he carried the manure out of the yard so that the smell might not offend; he trimmed his garden to make it tidy. A thing of beauty was this garden, a fit pleasance for a prince. It lay on high ground, extended a furlong in length, and its area was four acres; it was like a long plain. It contained trees of all kinds— apple, myrtle, pear, pomegranate, fig, and olive. On one side was a lofty vine, with ripe grapes mingled with the apples and pears, as if vying with their fruit. There were cultivated trees; there were also cypresses, laurels, planes, and pines. To these an ivy, in place of a grapevine, clung; its berries were large, and in darkness resembled the grapes. The fruit-bearing trees were in the interior, as if under protection; those that bore no fruit were ranged on the outside, like a palisade built by hand. A low hedge of dry stones ran round the whole. The garden was arranged according to a precise pattern, and the trunks were placed at regular intervals. But overhead the branches joined one another and their foliage intermingled; nature itself seemed a work of art. There were also beds of various flowers, some the earth's own sowing, some that man had sown. The roses, hyacinths, and lilies were cultivated by hand; the violets, narcissus, and pimpernel were the earth's gift. There was shade for summer, flowers for spring, fruit for autumn, and delight for every season.

The garden gave a fine view of the plain, where the grazing flocks could be seen; the sea also could be seen and the ships that sailed on it. The view added to the pleasures of the garden. Exactly in the middle of the garden, measuring by length and breadth, was a temple and altar of Dionysos. The altar was surrounded by ivy, the temple with clematis. The interior of the temple showed pictures of Dionysiac tales—Semele giving birth, Ariadne sleeping, Lycurgus fettered, Pentheos torn in pieces. There were shown also Indians vanquished and Tyrrhenian soldiers transformed. Everywhere were Satyrs treading and Bacchants dancing. Nor was Pan omitted; he was shown sitting on a rock and piping, as if he were providing a melody both for the treading and the dancing. Such was the garden, and Lamon ministered to it carefully, pruning away dead wood and propping its vines. He crowned the Dionysos, and dug channels to water the flowers. Daphnis had found a spring, which was used exclusively for the flowers; it was called Daphnis' spring.

Lamon also instructed Daphnis to fatten his goats to the best possible condition, for the master would surely wish to inspect them on his long deferred visit. As for the goats, Daphnis was confident that he would receive praise; he had doubled the number he had received, not one had been carried off by a wolf, and they were fatter than sheep. But because he wished to win the master's good will for his proposed marriage, Daphnis showed very great diligence and exerted every effort: he took his flock out very early, and brought them back very late. He watered them twice daily, and looked out for the richest pasturage. He remembered to get new bowls and many milk pails and larger cheese racks. So solicitous was he that he oiled the goats' horns and brushed their shag; one might fancy his a sacred flock of Pan. All his work on the goats was shared by Chloe, who neglected her own flock to have more time for Daphnis' charges, so that Daphnis thought it was her efforts that made his beasts so handsome.

While they were thus occupied a second messenger came from the city and ordered them to make their vintage as soon as possible. He himself would stay until the wine was made, and then return to the city to bring the master for the completion of the vintage. This Eudromos ("Mr. Goodrunner," a name given him because of his trade) they received very hospitably, and immediately began stripping the vines, bringing the clusters to the press, and pouring the must into the tuns. Some of the clusters on their vines they saved out, so that those who came out from the city might have some idea of the vintage and its pleasures. When Eudromos was ready to hurry back to the city Daphnis gave him many presents, such as a goatherd could give—compact cheeses, a late-born kid, and a woolly white goatskin to put on when he ran errands in the winter. Eudromos was well pleased and kissed Daphnis, and he promised to say a good word for him to the master. And so Eudromos set out with the friendliest of feelings, but Daphnis remained with Chloe in an agony of suspense. She for her part was very apprehensive, for he was very young and used to seeing only goats and hills and farmers and Chloe, and now for the first time he was going to see his master, who had previously been only a name. She was worried about Daphnis' behavior when he encountered the master, but her mind was also troubled about the marriage— would it prove an empty dream? Frequently did they kiss and frequently embrace, like plants that cling together; but their kisses were timid and their embraces sad-visaged, as if they feared the actual presence of the master or were avoiding his eyes. Then a new trouble added to their anxiety.

There was a certain truculent cowherd named Lampis, who had asked Dryas for Chloe's hand and to that end had made him many presents. When he got wind that Daphnis would marry her if the master should grant his consent, he sought for some expedient to put the master in a sour mood against him and Lamon. Knowing that the master was especially fond of the garden, he determined to ruin it and spoil its beauty. If he should cut down the trees he knew that the noise would betray him, and so he resolved to ruin the flowers. He waited for night, jumped over the hedge, and then dug up some of the flowers, crushed some, and stamped some down like a boar; then he got away unobserved. On the following morning Lamon went to the garden to water the flowers from the spring and saw the whole place devastated; the destruction was plainly a vandal's, not a thief's. Lamon tore his shirt in tatters and cried, "Ye gods!" so loudly that Myrtale dropped what she was doing and dashed out, and Daphnis let his goats go and ran up. When they saw the carnage they shrieked and wailed; this was a new kind of mourning—for flowers. It was for fear of their master that they wept, but even a stranger would weep at the sight. The place was dismantled, and only muddy ground was left. Blooms that had escaped the violent attack still flowered and shone and were beautiful even lying down. Upon them swarms of bees had settled, and their incessant buzzing was like a funeral dirge. Out of his consternation Lamon lamented: "Alas for my roses, how are they broken! Alas for my violets, how are they trodden underfoot! Alas for my hyacinth and narcissus, which some wicked mischief-maker has uprooted! The spring will return, but they will not bloom; the summer will come, but they will not flower; the autumn, but they will crown no one with garlands. And you, Lord Dionysos, did you not pity these poor flowers, with whom you live, at whom you look, from whom I have so frequently woven you garlands for your delight? How, how shall I now show this garden to my master? What will he say to me when he sees it? He will hang his old servant from some pine tree, like a Marsyas. Maybe he will hang Daphnis too, blaming his goats for the destruction." Now they no longer wept for the flowers, but for their own calamity, and their tears were the hotter. Chloe grieved at the thought of Daphnis hanging and prayed that their master might never come. She lived through heavy days of wretchedness, as if she already saw Daphnis under the scourge.

Night was just beginning when Eudromos reported to them that their elder master would arrive in three days, but that his son would come on the morrow. Now they deliberated about their misfortune and made Eudromos a participant in their councils. He had kind feelings for Daphnis and advised him first to confess the whole affair to the young master. He promised to support Daphnis' cause; having shared the young master's nursing, he had influence with him. The next day they did as he advised. Astylos came, on horseback, and with him, also on horseback, his toady. Astylos was but newly bearded, but Gnathon (for such was the toady's name) had long been shaving. Lamon, with Myrtale and Daphnis, fell at his feet, and besought him to pity an unfortunate old man and avert his father's anger from one who had done no wrong. Then he told him the whole story. Astylos pitied the suppliants, and when he had gone to the garden and had seen the ruin of the flowers, he said he would himself plead extenuation to his father and put the blame on his horses, which (he would say), being tethered there, had grown restive, broken loose, and crushed, trodden down, and uprooted the flowers. Thereupon Lamon and Myrtale called all good blessings down upon him, and Daphnis brought him presents—goats, cheeses, birds with their young, grapes on their vines, and apples on their boughs. Among the gifts was fragrant Lesbian wine, a delicious beverage.

Astylos thanked him warmly, and occupied himself with rabbit hunting, as was natural for a rich and pleasure-loving young man who had gone to the country to enjoy new amusement. Gnathon, a fellow who understood only eating, drinking himself drunk, and afterwards lechery—a fellow all jaws, belly, and the parts beneath—was very attentive when Daphnis brought his presents. He was naturally a pederast, and, having come upon such beauty as he had never seen in the city, he determined to make an attempt on Daphnis, and thought it easy to win a mere goatherd over. With this in mind he took no part in Astylos' hunt, but went where Daphnis was pasturing, on the pretext of watching the goats but actually to look at Daphnis. He softened him down by praising the goats and asking him to pipe some shepherd tune, and soon he said that he was in position to procure Daphnis' freedom. When he had thus made him more tractable, he waylaid him at night as he was driving the goats from pasture. First he ran up to him and kissed him, and then requested him to make his back accessible as the she-goats did for the males. Daphnis was slow in getting his drift, but then said that it was proper for she-goats to be leapt upon by males, but that no one had ever seen buck leaping upon buck, nor ram upon ram instead of ewe, nor cock upon cock instead of hen. Gnathon was prepared to use violence and raised his hands, but since he was sodden and scarcely able to stand upright Daphnis pushed him over and laid him sprawling. Then he scampered off like a puppy, leaving Gnathon lying there in greater want of a man to carry him home than of a handsome boy. For the future Daphnis kept out of his way, and pastured his flock now in one place and now in another, avoiding Gnathon and sticking near to Chloe. Nor was Gnathon persistent, for he had learned that Daphnis was rugged as well as handsome. Rather did he await an opportunity to speak about him to Astylos, from whom he hoped he would procure Daphnis as a gift, for that ingenuous young man was always ready to make generous presents. For the present no opportunity offered, for Dionysophantes and Cleariste had arrived, and there was a great commotion of pack animals, servants, men, and women; but he did set about composing a long erotic discourse.

Dionysophantes was now of middle age, but tall and handsome and able to hold his own even with young men. In wealth he had but few peers, in virtue none. On the first day of his arrival he offered sacrifice to the gods who preside over the countryside, Demeter and Dionysos and Pan and the Nymphs, and set out a large mixing bowl for all present to share. On the days following he inspected Lamon's work, and, seeing the fields well furrowed, the grapevines flourishing, and the garden in order (Astylos had taken the blame for the ruined flowers), he was highly pleased and praised Lamon and promised to set him free. After this he visited the herds also, to see the goats and their shepherd. Chloe ran away to the woods, for she was shy and timid before so great a crowd. But Daphnis stood his ground. He was girt in a shaggy goatskin and wore a newly stitched scrip slung from his shoulders; both hands were occupied, one holding new-pressed cheeses, and the other suckling kids. If ever Apollo served Laomedon as cowherd he must have looked as Daphnis now appeared. Daphnis himself said not a word, but bowed down, covered with blushes, and held out his gifts. But Lamon spoke: "This, master, is the keeper of your goats. You gave me fifty goats to pasture and two males; he has made of them a hundred goats and ten males. You see how sleek they are, how rich their wool, how sound their horns. He has even made them musical, for all their movements are regulated by the pipe."

Cleariste, who was present at this speech, desired a demonstration of what had been said, and bade Daphnis pipe as he was accustomed to do, and promised him a tunic, cloak, and shoes as a reward. Daphnis made them sit as in a theater, took his stand under the beech tree, and brought his pipe out of his scrip. At first he breathed into it very gently, and the goats stood still and raised their heads. Next he blew the grazing tune, and the goats put their heads down and grazed. Then he sounded a clear, sweet note, and they all lay down together. He piped a shrill strain, and the goats fled into the woods as if a wolf were on the rampage. After a little he sounded the recall, and they all emerged from their covert and trooped about his feet. No one had ever seen human servants so obedient to their master's orders. Everyone was amazed, but Cleariste most of all, and she pledged herself to pay the promised award to the goatherd who was not only handsome but musical as well. The party then returned to the steading and busied themselves with their lunch, and they sent Daphnis portions of their own food. Daphnis shared his dainties with Chloe. He took pleasure in the savor of city cooking, and was sanguine in his hope of persuading his master to consent to the marriage.

But the performance with the flock had fanned Gnathon's fire, and he thought life not worth living unless he could succeed with Daphnis. He watched for Astylos to go walking in the garden, and then took him to the temple of Dionysos and kissed his feet and hands. When Astylos inquired why he did so and bade him speak, with an oath that he would serve his need, Gnathon said: "Master, your Gnathon is done for. I used to be in love only with your table, I used to swear that nothing was lovelier than elderly wine, I used to say your cooking was better than all the pretty boys in Mytilene—now I think that only Daphnis is beautiful. I do not savor your luxurious viands of which such an abundance—meat, fish, pastries—is served up every day. I would liefer be a goat and browse on grass and leaves if only I could hear Daphnis' piping and be in his charge. Save your own Gnathon, vanquish love, the invincible. If not, I swear to you by my own deity that I will take a dagger and, when I have filled my belly with food, kill myself in front of Daphnis'

angry arch. He questioned Lamon and bade him speak the truth and not invent fictions in order to keep his son at home. Lamon persevered, and swore by all the gods, and offered to undergo torture to prove whether he were lying. With Cleariste as his assessor Dionysophantes scrutinized the tale. "Why should Lamon lie when he is to receive two goatherds for one? How could a rustic invent such a tale? Is it not a priori unlikely that so handsome a son should be born of such an old man and such a plain woman?"

They decided to conjecture no further but examine the tokens, to see whether they bespoke a wealthy and noble fortune. Myrtale had gone off to fetch the articles kept in an old scrip, and when they were brought Dionysophantes looked at them first. When he saw the little purple cloak, the gold brooch, and the ivory-hilted sword he cried, "Lord Zeus!" and called his wife to look. When she saw, she too cried out: "Ye dear Fates, are not these the things we exposed with our own child? Is it not to this neighborhood that we ordered Sophrosyne to carry them? They are no different, but the very same. My dear husband, the child is ours. Daphnis is your son, and has been tending his own father's goats."

While she was still speaking and Dionysophantes was caressing the tokens and weeping for excess of joy, Astylos, understanding that Daphnis was his brother, flung off his cloak and ran to the garden, wishing to be the first to kiss him. When Daphnis saw him running, with others behind him, and shouting, "Daphnis!" he thought that it was in order to seize him that he ran, and so he flung down his scrip and pipe and made for the sea, with the intention of hurling himself down from the high rock. And perhaps (strange thought!) Daphnis found would have been lost, had not Astylos grasped the situation and called out: "Stop, Daphnis, do not be afraid! I am your brother, and your parents are they who were hitherto your masters. Lamon has just now told us about the she-goat and shown us the tokens. Turn around and look, see how happy and smiling our faces are. And give me the first kiss: I swear by the Nymphs that I am not deceiving you." These oaths barely prevailed upon Daphnis to halt, and he awaited Astylos, who was running, and kissed him when he came. While he was kissing him the rest of the crowd swept up—menservants, maidservants, the father himself, and his mother with him. All embraced and kissed him with happy tears. He greeted his father and mother before all the others, and, as if he had always known them, clung to their breasts and would not leave their embrace—so quickly does nature assert its rights. Even Chloe was momentarily forgotten. Daphnis now returned to the farmstead, put on costly dress, sat down by his real father, and heard him tell the following story:

"I married, my children, when I was quite young, and in a short time became, as I thought, a happy father. First a son was born to me, next a daughter, and the third was you, Astylos. I thought my brood sufficient, and the child that was born after them I exposed; these articles I exposed with it not as tokens for recognition but as burial ornaments. But the designs of fortune were other. My elder son and my daughter died of one disease on the same day, but by the providence of the gods you, Daphnis, were saved, to be a further stay for our old age. Do not bear me ill will for having once exposed you; I did not do so with a willing mind. Nor do you, Astylos, be grieved at receiving part instead of all of my estate. For people of sound mind no possession is more precious than a brother. Love one another; as for wealth, you can vie with princes. I shall leave you extensive lands, many deft servants, gold, silver, and the other chattels of the rich. Only this particular place I reserve for Daphnis, together with Lamon and Myrtale and the goats which he himself has pastured." While he was yet speaking Daphnis leapt up and said, "Father, thank you for reminding me. I am going to take the goats to water. They are surely thirsty, waiting for the signal of my pipe, and here I am, sitting still." All laughed heartily at the new master's still wishing to be the goatherd. Another servant was sent to attend to the goats, and the company offered sacrifice to Zeus, the savior, and joined in a jolly banquet. The only one who did not come to the banquet was Gnathon, who was afraid and remained in the temple of Dionysos all that day and night as a suppliant.

Quickly did the report spread abroad that Dionysophantes had found a son and that Daphnis, the goatherd, was discovered to be the master of his fields; and so in the morning there was a great concourse from all quarters, to offer felicitations to the young man and bring gifts to his father. Among these Dryas, Chloe's foster father, was the first. Dionysophantes detained them all to share in the festivities upon the joyous occasion. There was got ready quantities of wine and wheaten bread, marsh fowl, suckling pigs, and various sweetmeats; and many sacrifices were offered to the local deities. There Daphnis collected all his pastoral implements, and distributed them as votive offerings to the gods. To Dionysos he dedicated his scrip and skin, to Pan his pipe and transverse flute, to the Nymphs his crook and the pails which he himself had fashioned. But habit is more agreeable than unexpected prosperity, and he wept as he parted with each of these articles. Nor did he dedicate the pails before he milked into them once more, nor the skin before he tried it on, nor the pipe before he blew it. All of these things he kissed, and he spoke to his goats, and called the males by name. He also drank from the spring, for he had so often done so with Chloe. He had not yet confessed his love, but watched for a proper occasion.

While Daphnis was occupied with his offerings, this is what happened to Chloe: As was natural, she sat crying: "Daphnis has forgotten me. He is dreaming of some rich match. Why did I bid him swear by the goats instead of the Nymphs? He has deserted the goats and Chloe too. Not even while sacrificing to the Nymphs and Pan did he desire to see Chloe. Perhaps he has found his mother's waiting women preferable to me. Good-by to him. I shall not live." While she was still immersed in such dreams the cowherd Lampis with a rustic band suddenly came up and seized her; he thought that Daphnis would not now marry her, and that Dryas would welcome his suit. And so she was carried off, wailing pitifully; a bystander informed Nape, she Dryas, and Dryas Daphnis. Daphnis went out of his wits. He did not dare speak to his father, and yet could not contain himself, and so he went out to the garden and lamented: "Ah, bitter discovery! How much better to be a shepherd! How much happier I was as a slave! Then I could see Chloe, then kiss her; but now Lampis has snatched her and gone off, and when night comes he will sleep with her. But here I am drinking and feasting; it is in vain that I swore by Pan and the goats and the Nymphs."

These plaints that Daphnis uttered were overheard by Gnathon, who was lurking in the garden. Thinking this offered an occasion for reconciliation with Daphnis, he took a band of Astylos' young men and went in pursuit of Dryas, whom he bade guide him to Lampis' steading. He proceeded there on the double, and overtook Lampis just as he was dragging Chloe into his house. Her he freed, and he gave Lampis' rustic band a drubbing. Lampis himself he was eager to tie up and bring as a prisoner of war, but Lampis was too quick and got away. Having accomplished his enterprise, Gnathon returned in the early hours of the night. Dionysophantes was already asleep, but Daphnis he found in the garden, sleepless and weeping. Gnathon delivered Chloe into his hands and told him the whole incident. Then he begged him not to keep a grudge against a man who would prove a useful servant, and not to deprive him of the table without which he would perish of hunger. Seeing Chloe and holding her in his arms, Daphnis forgave Gnathon because of his benefaction, and made apologies to Chloe for his neglect.

Now they consulted together and decided to marry secretly and to reveal the secret to no one except her mother. Dryas did not agree; he thought Daphnis' father should be told, and himself promised to procure his consent. When day broke he took Chloe's tokens in his scrip and went to Dionysophantes and Cleariste, whom he found sitting in the garden. Astylos and Daphnis himself were also present, and when silence obtained, he began to speak: "A necessity like Lamon's bids me to speak things hitherto unspoken. Chloe, here, I did not beget, nor did I nurse her; others gave her birth, and a ewe nursed her as she lay in the grotto of the Nymphs. I myself saw her there, and seeing, marveled, and marveling, I brought her up. Witness her beauty, which is unlike our state; witness, too, her tokens, which are richer than beseems a shepherd. Examine these things, and seek out the girl's relatives; perhaps her position is worthy of Daphnis." Not without design did Dryas drop this last remark, nor did Dionysophantes fail to notice it. He looked at Daphnis, and when he saw him turn pale and shed a furtive tear, he quickly discerned the lover. But as he was more concerned for his own son than for a strange girl, he examined what Dryas had said with the closest scrutiny. But when he saw the token that had been brought—the gilt shoes, the anklets, and the headband—he summoned Chloe to himself and bade her take heart: a husband she already had, and soon she would find her father and mother. Cleariste now took her and dressed her as became her son's wife. Dionysophantes drew Daphnis aside, and asked him whether Chloe were still a maid, and Daphnis swore that nothing more than kisses and pledges had passed between them. Dionysophantes was pleased with these assurances, and made them recline together at table.

Now could it be seen what beauty is when it receives proper adornment. Chloe dressed, with her hair combed and face washed, seemed so much handsomer to everyone that even Daphnis scarcely recognized her. Even without the tokens anyone would have sworn that Dryas was not the father of such a girl. He was, nevertheless, present, and Nape with him at the feast, and at a special couch, he had as his fellow diners Lamon and Myrtale. On the following days victims were again sacrificed and mixing bowls set out, and Chloe too dedicated her implements—pipe, scrip, skin, milk pails. She also mingled wine into the fountain in the grotto, for near it she had been nurtured and in it had often bathed. She also crowned the grave of the ewe, which Dryas pointed out to her. And she piped once more to her flock; and then piped in prayer to the Nymphs that she should find the parents who exposed her worthy of her union with Daphnis.

When the party had had enough of rustic festivities they decided to return to the city, to seek Chloe's parents and to defer the marriage no longer. Early in the morning their baggage was packed. To Dryas they gave another three thousand drachmas, and to Lamon a half share in the harvest and vintage of his fields, and also the goats, goatherds, four yoke of oxen, winter clothing, and freedom for himself and his wife. After this they proceeded to Mytilene, traveling in grand style with horses and carriages. Arriving at night, they escaped the notice of the citizenry for the moment; but on the following day a crowd of men and women gathered about their doors. The men felicitated Dionysophantes on the discovery of his son, and the more ardently when they saw Daphnis' beauty. The women congratulated Cleariste on bringing home both a son and a bride. Even the women were impressed by the unparalleled beauty which Chloe revealed. The whole city was in a bustle over the young man and the maiden, and were already calling the marriage blessed. They hoped that the family of the girl would be found worthy of her beauty, and many of the richest ladies prayed the gods that they themselves might be credited with being the mother of so beautiful a daughter.

To Dionysophantes, who had fallen into a deep sleep after his anxious thoughts, the following dream appeared. The Nymphs appeared to be requesting Eros to give them his consent for the marriage. Eros slackened his bow, laid aside his quiver, and bade Dionysophantes invite all the gentry of Mytilene to a banquet, and when he had filled the last mixing bowl, to display the tokens to each guest, and then raise the hymeneal chant. Dionysophantes rose early in the morning, when he had seen and heard this, and ordered the preparation of a sumptuous feast of all the delicacies of land and sea, and even of lakes and rivers; all the Mytilenean gentry he invited to be his guests. When it was dark and the mixing bowl from which libation is made to Hermes was brought in, a servant carried the tokens around on a silver charger from left to right, and exhibited them to each guest.

No one acknowledged them until a certain Megacles, who, because of his age, was reclining in the last place, recognized them when he saw them, and cried out in a loud and animated voice, "What is this I see? What has happened to you, my daughter? Are you alive? Or did some shepherd merely find these things and carry them away? I beg you, Dionysophantes, tell me, where did you get these tokens of my child? Do not grudge me a discovery, now you have Daphnis." Dionysophantes bade him first tell the story of the exposure, and Megacles, not abating the intensity of his voice said, "In time past my livelihood was scant, for what I possessed I spent lavishly upon my state obligations to equip choruses and fit out battleships. While such was my condition a little daughter was born to me. I shrank from bringing her up in poverty, and so adorned her with these tokens and exposed her, being aware that many people are eager to become parents even after this fashion. And so she was laid in the grotto of the Nymphs and entrusted to those deities. Upon me wealth has been pouring daily, and I have no heir, for I was never so fortunate as to become the father even of a girl. But, as if to make a mockery of me, by night the gods keep sending me dreams which signify that a sheep will make me a father."

Then Dionysophantes cried out in a voice louder than Megacles', and sprang from his place, and brought Chloe in very beautifully attired and said, "This is the child you exposed. By the providence of the Nymphs a ewe suckled this maiden for you, as a she-goat did Daphnis for me. Take your tokens and your daughter; take her and give her as a bride to Daphnis. Both have we exposed, both have we found; both have been cared for by Pan, the Nymphs, and Eros." Megacles approved of what had been said; he sent for his wife Rhode, and held Chloe to his bosom. They took their rest in that house, for Daphnis had sworn that he would part with Chloe to no one, not even to her own father.

When day dawned, upon the consent of all, they returned to the country. Daphnis and Chloe had begged to do so, for they could not endure their sojourn in the city; and the parents deemed it right that the marriage be celebrated in a rustic manner. When they arrived at Lamon's cottage they introduced Dryas to Megacles, and to Rhode they presented Nape; and then sumptuous preparations were made for the festivities. Her father gave Chloe away in the presence of the Nymphs, and along with many other offerings he dedicated the tokens to them. To Dryas he presented money to complete the sum of ten thousand drachmas. But Dionysophantes, since the day was fine, strewed couches of green leaves on the ground in front of the grotto, and he invited all the villagers to recline there and regaled them luxuriously. There were present Lamon and Myrtale, Dryas and Nape, Dorcon's kinsmen, Philetas and his sons, and Chromis and Lycainion; even Lampis had been pardoned and was there. As beseemed such a banquet, the entertainment was all of a rustic pastoral kind. One sang the song the reapers sing, another cracked the jokes the vintagers crack. Philetas blew his pipe and Lampis his flute; Dryas and Lamon danced. Chloe and Daphnis kissed one another. Even the goats grazed nearby, as if they too shared in the festivities. To the city folk this was not very agreeable, but Daphnis called the bucks by name, and gave them green leaves to eat, and held them by the horns and kissed them.

And not only then, but as long as they lived, for the greater part of the time Daphnis and Chloe led a pastoral life. They revered the gods, Nymphs, Pan, and Eros, they acquired numerous herds of sheep and goats, they thought fruit and milk the sweetest fare. Their male child they put to a goat to suckle, and their little daughter, who was the younger, they made to nurse from a ewe: him they called Philopoimen, her Agele. In this manner of life and in this spot they grew old together. They decorated the grotto, dedicated statues, and established an altar to Eros the Shepherd. Instead of his pine they gave Pan a temple to live in, and called it Pan the Warrior's.

But these things they did and these names they gave in later years. Upon that occasion, when night fell, the entire company escorted them to their bridal chamber, some playing pipes, some flutes, and others raising large torches. And when they came near the door, they sang out in shrill and harsh tones, as if they were breaking ground with three-pronged forks, not chanting a hymeneal. Daphnis and Chloe lay down together naked. They embraced and kissed one another, and were no less wakeful than owls. And Daphnis performed as Lycainion had taught him, and for the first time Chloe learned that their pastime in the woods had been mere pastoral play.

An Ephesian Tale

BY XENOPHON

At Ephesus *lived a man named Lycomedes, a principal* figure in that city. He had to wife Themiste, who was also a native Ephesian, and their son was Habrocomes, a prodigy of beauty unrivaled in Ionia or elsewhere. This Habrocomes grew handsomer day by day, and the qualities of his soul kept equal pace with the beauty of his person. He was diligent in every form of culture, and practiced the various arts; his training included the chase and horsemanship and fencing. By all the Ephesians was he cherished, and likewise by the inhabitants of other parts of Asia; all expected that he would one day bring great distinction to his city. They honored the lad as he were a god, and indeed some there were who bowed down when they saw him and offered him prayer. Now the youth conceived a high opinion of himself; he vaunted himself upon the merits of his spirit, but much more upon the beauty of his person. Whatever the world counted beautiful he despised as inferior and indeed negligible in comparison with himself. Nothing that the world had to show or tell did Habrocomes deem worthy of himself. And if any spoke of some lad as handsome or some maid as comely he laughed at their ignorance; the only true beauty, of course, was himself. He even denied that Eros was a god; nay, he dismissed him as a cipher and banished him utterly. He declared that no one at all had ever been mastered by love or become subject to that "god" unless he wished to be. And if ever he saw a sanctuary or statue of Eros he ridiculed it and boasted that he was handsomer than any Eros. Actually that seemed the case, for wherever Habrocomes came into view no statue seemed beautiful, no image was admired.

At this Eros waxed wroth; jealous is that divinity, and to the proud inexorable. He sought for some device to snare that lad, for even to the god he seemed hard to overreach. He accoutered himself, therefore, cap-a-pie, armed himself with his powerful love philters, and marched against Habrocomes. The local festival of Artemis was in progress, and the procession moved from the city to the shrine; the distance was seven furlongs. Usage required that all the maidens of the region, richly attired, and all the lads of Habrocomes' age join in the procession. Habrocomes was now sixteen years of age and already classed a cadet, and he played the principal role in the cortege. A great concourse had assembled for the spectacle; there were many Ephesians and many visitors, for it was customary for bridegrooms to be found for maidens at that festival, and wives for the cadets. And so the procession moved past. In the van were the sacred objects, the torches, the baskets, and the incense. Following these were horses and dogs and hunting gear; there was some display of military equipment, but more of the arts of peace.

The girls in the procession were all decked out as if to meet lovers. Of the band of maidens the leader was Anthia, daughter of the Ephesians Megamedes and Evippe. Anthia was a prodigy of loveliness and far surpassed the other maidens. Her age was fourteen, and she had bloomed into mature shapeliness. Her grooming enhanced her charm. Her hair was yellow, for the most part loose, but with some tresses braided, and it stirred at the movement of the breeze. Her eyes were lively, shining sometimes like a girl's, sometimes severe, as of a chaste goddess. Her dress was a frock of purple, fitted down to the knee and hanging loose over the arms. Her wrap was a fawn skin, and a quiver hung from her shoulder. She carried bow and javelins, and dogs followed at her heels. Time and again when the Ephesians saw her in the sacred precinct they bowed down as to Artemis. And now too when Anthia came into view the entire multitude cried out in astonishment; some of the spectators asserted that she was the very goddess, others declared she was a replica fashioned by the goddess. But all did obeisance to her and bowed down and called her parents blessed. From all the spectators there arose cheers for Anthia the beautiful, and of all the maidens in the procession only Anthia was spoken of. But however beautiful the spectacle of the maidens had been, they were forgotten completely when Habrocomes appeared with the cadets. The people gazed at him, were smitten by the sight, and cried out, "Habrocomes is beautiful!" "None is so fair!" "He is the image of a beautiful god!" There were some too who now added, "What a marriage that of Habrocomes and Anthia would be!" This was the first stage of Eros' campaign. Each of the young people soon heard reports of the other. Anthia was eager to see Habrocomes, and Habrocomes, who had been insensible to love, now wished to see Anthia.

When the procession was finished the entire multitude approached the shrine to offer sacrifice, and the order of the march was broken up. Now there was no distinction of sexes; cadets and maidens mingled, and could eye one another. Anthia was captivated by Habrocomes, and Habrocomes was laid low by Eros. His stare was fixed on the girl, and though he would withdraw his eyes he could not; the god pressed him hard and held him fast. Anthia for her part was no less smitten. With her whole being she caught the beauty of Habrocomes, which flowed into her wide open eyes. And now she disregarded maidenly modesty; she murmured words for Habrocomes to overhear and uncovered as much of her person as she could for Habrocomes to see. And Habrocomes gave himself wholly to the sight; the god's bound prisoner was he. When the sacrifice was finished they parted from one another, sadly and with regret at the brevity of the encounter. Wishing mightily to look upon one another, ever and again they turned about, and halted, and discovered many pretexts for delay. But it was when each arrived home that they realized the depth of their distress. Each was overwhelmed by the impression the other had left, in each was love's flame kindled. During the remainder of the day their agitation grew, and when they retired to sleep they found themselves in deep anguish. Upon each love pressed irresistibly.

Habrocomes pulled his hair and ripped his clothes. "Ah me for my troubles!" he said. "What, unlucky that I am, has happened to me? Till now I was that stalwart Habrocomes, the champion who despised Eros, the man who reviled the god, and now I am taken prisoner and vanquished and forced into slavery to a girl; now another seems fairer to me than myself, and I acknowledge that Eros is a god. Ah, but I am a spineless coward! Shall I not now resist, shall I not show courage and endure? Shall I not be handsomer than Eros? Now must I overcome that god who is only a cipher! Fair is the maiden, granted; but what then? To your eyes, Habrocomes, Anthia is comely; but if you are so determined, not to *yourself*. This then must be my doctrine; Eros must never be my master." So he said, but the god pressed him the more vehemently, and dragged him, though he resisted, and tormented him, though he was otherwise minded. And when he could withstand no longer he flung himself down upon the ground, and said, "Thou hast conquered, Eros; great is thy trophy for victory over chaste Habrocomes. Thou seest him suppliant before thy feet. Preserve him who seeks asylum of thee, who art master of all creatures. Do not abandon me, nor too strictly punish my foolhardiness. Out of ignorance, Eros, I behaved arrogantly in thy domain. But now give me Anthia! Show thyself a god not only severe to the recalcitrant but also benevolent to the vanquished." So he said, but Eros continued angry and planned how he might make Habrocomes render full payment for his insults.

Anthia too was in deep distress, and when she could bear it no longer she roused herself in an effort to conceal her state. "Unhappy that I am," said she, "what has come over me? I am a maid, and love beyond what suits my age; I am tormented by pains that are strange and unbecoming to a girl. I am mad with love for Habrocomes, who is handsome indeed, but exceedingly proud. What will be the limit of this passion, what the end of this woe? Formidable is the man I love, and I am a maid, kept under ward. Whom shall I find to be my help? To whom can I confide my distress? Where shall I see Habrocomes?" Thus did each of the two lament the whole night through. Their mutual likenesses they kept before their eyes, and each stamped upon his own soul the molded image of the other.

When day broke Habrocomes went to his usual exercises, and the maid went, as her custom was, to minister to the goddess. Their sufferings through the night had left their bodies wearied, their eyes listless, their complexions wan. This state continued long, and they obtained no solace. During this while they passed whole days in the temple of the goddess, gazing upon one another but constrained and afraid to reveal the truth to one another. Only so much: Habrocomes would groan and weep and would make his prayers most pitiful when the girl was within hearing. Anthia endured like suffering, but was afflicted with this great distress: whenever she observed other maidens or women gazing upon the youth (and all her sex did gaze fondly upon Habrocomes) her suffering was plain to see, for she feared she would be outdone in his esteem. But their prayers to the goddess were common to both; without their being aware of it their petitions were identical.

As time went on the young man languished. His frame was emaciated and his spirit was so crushed that Lycomedes and Themiste fell into despair; what had befallen Habrocomes they knew not, but what they could see filled them with apprehension. In similar dread were Megamedes and Evippe for the fate of Anthia: they observed that her beauty was drooping, but the cause of the calamity was not apparent. At length they fetched soothsayers and holy men to Anthia, to find some solution for the trouble. These busily offered divers sacrifices and poured divers libations and pronounced certain unintelligible syllables in order to appease, as they said, certain demonic powers, and they feigned that the malady was a visitation of the gods of the nether world. For Habrocomes, too, did Lycomedes and his friends offer many sacrifices and prayers. But no solution for their malady was vouchsafed either; nay, the fire of love burned yet fiercer. They lay then there, the two of them sick, their disease now so critical that nothing less than speedy death was looked for, and they were yet unable to give utterance to their own calamity. Finally the fathers of both sent to consult the divine oracle for the cause of the disease and the means for its relief.

The shrine of Apollo in Colophon was but a short distance away; the crossing from Ephesus was a matter of only eighty furlongs. When the emissaries dispatched by the two parents arrived there they besought the god to render a true oracle; for this purpose had they come. And the god delivered a single oracle in common to both, in meter, in form as follows:

Why yearn ye to learn the end of disease or its beginning?
Both a single malady holds fast, and hence the solution issues.
Yet perceive I for these twain fearful suffering and toils protracted.
Both shall flee o'er the brine pursued by pirates,
They shall be laden with fetters by men who live by the sea.
For both a bridal chamber will serve as a tomb, and fire the destroyer;
And by the floods of the river Nile upon holy Isis
The savior goddess you will thereafter bestow rich gifts.
But after their woes their lot grants a fortune that is better.

When the oracle was brought to Ephesus the fathers forthwith fell into a quandary, being at a complete loss to know what the evil might be. To divine the dark sayings of the god they were not able, nor could they guess the meaning of the malady or the flight or the fetters or the tomb or the river or the help the goddess would vouchsafe. After long deliberation it seemed to them best to mitigate the oracle so far as in them lay and to join their children in marriage, for such seemed the will of the god in the oracle he had rendered. This they determined to do, and they resolved to send the young people away to sojourn abroad for a time after their marriage.

The city was now filled with feasting, everything was bedecked with garlands, and the intended marriage was widely bruited abroad. Felicitations were offered on all hands—to the young man for the excellent wife he would lead home, and to the young woman for the splendid spouse she would enjoy. When Habrocomes learned of the oracle and of the marriage, he was greatly rejoiced at coming into possession of Anthia; the predictions frightened him not at all, for his present happiness seemed to him to overweigh any evil. And after the same fashion Anthia rejoiced that she would possess Habrocomes; she cared little for the flight and other troubles, having in Habrocomes solace for any future tribulations. When the season for the marriage was come, vigils were celebrated the night through and numerous victims were sacrificed to the goddess. And when these rites were done and night was come (but Habrocomes and Anthia thought it very tardy), they conducted the girl to the bridal chamber with torches, chanting the hymeneal hymn, and they pronounced propitious blessings upon them, and introduced them to their bridal couch. The fashion of their bridal chamber was as follows: the couch of gold was spread with purple coverings, and over the couch was a canopy of Babylonian stuff richly embroidered: there were sportive Cupids, some ministering to Aphrodite (Aphrodite herself was represented in a figure), some riding mounted on sparrows, some were twining wreaths, and some were bearing flowers. These designs occupied one side of the canopy. On the other there was Ares, without his weapons, but finely dressed, as if to meet his beloved Aphrodite, wearing a wreath and draped in a cape. Eros was conducting him on his way, carrying a lighted torch. Under this canopy they caused Anthia to recline, after they brought her to Habrocomes, and then they closed the doors.

Their emotions were identical. They were able neither to address a word one to the other, nor to look upon each other's eyes; but they lay there languid with delight, modest, timid, breathing rapidly. Their bodies trembled, their souls were agitated. Finally Habrocomes collected himself, and embraced Anthia. She wept: 'twas her soul that sent forth those tears in token of her yearning. Then said Habrocomes, "O Night most fondly desired and at long last won, after the miseries of so many earlier nights! Darling, dearer to me than light, blissful beyond all utterance, you hold in your arms the man who loves you; with him may it be vouchsafed you to live and to die, a chaste wife." When he had so spoken he kissed her, and collected her tears, and to him those tears seemed more delicious than any nectar and a more potent anodyne than any drug. She in turn murmured some words to him, and said, "Am I truly fair in your sight, Habrocomes? Inferior as I am to your beauty, do I still please you? Timid and fearful lad, how long will you delay your love-making? How much time will you waste? From my own anguish I know what you must have suffered. But see, now, take these my tears, and let your pretty hair drink up this potion of love. Let us cleave to one another and commingle, let us drench these garlands in one another's tears, that they too may join in love with us." When she had said all this she fondled his face and drew all his hair to touch her eyes; and then she removed the wreaths, and applied her lips to his in a close kiss, and the thoughts that were in the mind of each they transmitted through their lips from the soul of one to the soul of the other. And when she kissed his eyes she said, "Ah, ye twain that have so often inflicted pain upon me, ye that first thrust the goad into my spirit, ye that were then cruel but now filled with love, well have ye served me, passing well have ye conveyed love of me into the soul of Habrocomes. Therefore do I love you passing well, and to you I will apply close these eyes of mine, now the handmaids of Habrocomes. Ever may ye see as ye see this day: show no other fair to Habrocomes, and let no other lad seem handsome in my sight. Now ye possess the souls which yourselves have set aflame: guard and preserve them in like fashion." Such things she spoke, and then, clinging one to the other, they went to their rest and plucked the first fruits of Aphrodite. The whole night they spent in eager rivalry with one another, contending which should appear the more ardent lover.

When day shone forth they arose happier and with better cheer, because they had attained mutual enjoyment of the bliss for which they had long yearned. All of life seemed to them a festival, all was filled with good cheer, so that the oracle slipped into forgetfulness. But fate slipped not into forgetfulness, nor was that god negligent who determined these things. When a little time had passed the fathers resolved to send the young people from the city, as they had previously decided. Their purpose was to explore another country and other cities and, so far as this was possible, to mitigate the oracle of the god by absenting themselves from Ephesus for a season. All things, then, were made ready against their departure; a stately ship and suitable seamen to sail it was got ready, and supplies were stowed aboard—a great abundance and variety of clothing, much silver and gold, and huge stocks of provisions. Before the voyage sacrifices were offered to Artemis; prayers were uttered by all the folk, and all shed tears, as if they were about to be separated from children that belonged to the whole people. It was for Egypt that the voyage had been prepared. When the day of departure was come, a crowd of menservants and maidservants [embarked with their young masters], and when the vessel was about to weigh anchor the whole multitude of the Ephesians attended to see them off, and there were many [strangers] also, with torches and sacrifices. Lycomedes and Themiste, in the meanwhile, when they recalled the whole series of events —the oracle, their son, his departure—collapsed to the ground in their despair. Megamedes and Evippe shared the same distress, indeed, but nevertheless took better heart when they reflected on the final issue of the oracle. And now the shouts of the sailors rang out, and the hawsers were loosed, and the skipper took his post, and the ship began to move. There was a great outcry, in which were mingled voices from the shore and those on the ship. These cried out, "Dearest children, shall we who begat you ever see you again?" And those, "Dear parents, shall we ever see you again?" There were tears and lamentations, and each called upon his own kindred by name, leaving the name as it were a memorial for one another. Now Megamedes took a chalice in hand, and as he poured libation he prayed so that he might be heard by those on shipboard, saying, "Children, may you prosper greatly and avoid the hard sayings of the oracle; may the Ephesians receive you safe home again, and may you recover your own beloved country. If any different issue should befall, know that we·shall not continue in life. The path upon which we send you is sad indeed, but inevitable." Even as he was speaking a burst of tears checked his utterance. The parents then returned to the city, the multitude encouraging them to be of good heart.

But Habrocomes and Anthia lay intertwined in one another's arms, brooding over many things in their minds. They pitied their parents, yearned for their homeland, dreaded the oracle, were apprehensive of the voyage; but for all these things their sufficient solace was that they voyaged together. That day they had the advantage of a tail wind, and with good sailing they made Samos, the sacred island of Hera. There they offered sacrifice and took their dinner and said many prayers, and when night came on they continued their journey. Again sailing was favorable, and they had much conversation with one another. "Will it be vouchsafed us to live our lives out with one another?" Then indeed did Habrocomes fetch a deep sigh when he recalled what fate awaited him, and he said, "Anthia, dearer far to me than life, may it indeed be our lot to be blessed and preserved together. But if it be fated for us to undergo affliction

by Xenophon 79

and somehow be separated one from the other, let us swear an oath to one another, dearly beloved, you that you will abide chaste unto me and never tolerate another man, and I that I shall never consort with another woman." When Anthia heard this she exclaimed, "Why this, Habrocomes? Can you believe that if I am separated from you I can take thought for a man and for marriage when I cannot even live at all without you? I solemnly invoke to witness our great ancestral goddess, great Diana of the Ephesians, and this sea upon which we sail, and that divinity who has so well implanted in us passionate love for one another, that if I am separated from you even for any short shrift of time, I shall not live, shall not longer look upon the sun." So spoke Anthia, and Habrocomes too swore, and the circumstances and occasion lent solemnity to their oaths. Meanwhile their ship skirted Cos and Cnidos, and then the large and fair island of Rhodes hove into view. There they must needs disembark, for the sailors declared that they must draw water and themselves take rest in preparation for the long voyage that faced them.

And so the ship made land at Rhodes and the sailors disembarked. Habrocomes, too, went ashore, holding Anthia by the hand. Astonished at the beauty of these two the Rhodians gathered in a crowd, and none who saw them passed in silence. Some said that these were divinities come to sojourn on the island; others bowed down to them and sought their favor. Quickly through the entire city the names of Habrocomes and Anthia were spread abroad. Public prayers were addressed to them and many victims were sacrificed, and their arrival was celebrated as a festive day. They for their part toured the whole city; in the shrine of the Sun they deposited a golden panoply as a votive offering, and inscribed upon it this memorial of their dedication:

> These golden gifts to thee have strangers dedicated—
> Anthia and Habrocomes, townsmen of sacred Ephesus.

When they had made this offering and had sojourned in the island for some days, at the insistence of the crew they embarked again; the ship was provisioned, and the entire multitude of the Rhodians escorted them to their sailing.

At first they were borne along with a prospering wind, and they took great pleasure in the voyage. That day and the night following they traversed the sea called Egyptian, but on the next day the wind dropped into a dead calm. The sailors were idle and took to drink; then came drunkenness and the beginning of the oracle's fulfillment. Habrocomes had a vision of a woman standing over him, fearful to behold, of stature larger than human, and clothed in a scarlet robe. She seemed to him to set the ship afire; the others, it seemed, perished, while he and Anthia swam free. As soon as he saw this vision Habrocomes was deeply disturbed; he foresaw that his dream would have some dreadful issue, and dreadful indeed were the events that transpired.

It happened that pirates, who were Phoenicians by race, had had their large galley moored near them at Rhodes. They were numerous and rugged, and pretended that they carried merchandise. These men learned that the Ephesian vessel was laden with gold and silver and many valuable slaves, and so they determined to attack it, put to death those who should offer resistance, and carry the others and the rest of the valuables off to Phoenicia for sale. The Ephesians they despised as incapable of strenuous resistance. The leader of the pirates was called Corymbos; he was a young man of large frame and fierce aspect, and his hair was rough and unkempt. When the pirates had laid their plans, at first they sailed quietly near Habrocomes' ship; but then, when it was about noon, and the crew was lying about sluggish with drink and idleness, some asleep and some helpless, Corymbos and his men urged their galley ahead with great speed. When they drew alongside they leapt upon the vessel fully armed and brandishing naked swords. Thereupon some flung themselves into the sea, surprised out of their wits, and perished; others who showed resistance were massacred. But Habrocomes and Anthia ran to the pirate Corymbos and said, "Keep the property and ourselves as slaves, master, but spare our lives and do not murder those who willingly submit to you. Do not so, we beseech you, by the sea itself, by your right hand. Take us whithersoever you will, sell us who are your slaves; only take pity and dispose of us to the same master."

When Corymbos heard this he issued orders immediately for

the slaughter to cease, and when he had transshipped the more valuable freight, including Habrocomes and Anthia and a few selected slaves, he set fire to the vessel, and all the others were consumed in flames. To carry them all Corymbos was not able, and he saw that it was not safe. Pitiful indeed was the spectacle, some being carried off in the galley, others consumed in the burning ship, stretching their hands out and wailing. Some cried out, "Whither, masters, are you bound? What shores will receive you and in what city do you dwell?" Others said, "Blessed are those who will happily die before they have tasted chains, before they have looked upon bondage to robbers." Amid such cries some were haled off, some devoured by the flames. Meanwhile the tutor of Habrocomes, now an old man of venerable aspect and pitiful because of his age, when he could not endure to see Habrocomes carried off, flung himself into the sea and swam to overtake the galley, crying as he went, "Where will you leave me, my child, the old man, your tutor? Where are you off to, Habrocomes? Kill me yourself, wretch that I am, and bury me. How can I live without you?" Thus he said, and at length, despairing of seeing Habrocomes any longer, he gave himself up to the waves and died. To Habrocomes this was the most harrowing thing of all. He stretched his hands out to the old man and besought the pirates to take him up, but they paid no attention and sailed on. In three days they made land at Tyre, the Phoenician city where the pirates had their dwellings. Their booty they took not to the city itself but to a nearby retreat that belonged to the chief of the band, Apsyrtos by name. Him Corymbos served as lieutenant for wages and a share of what was taken.

In the course of the voyage Corymbos had seen Habrocomes daily and had fallen violently in love with him, and his familiar association with the young man had added fuel to his passion. During the voyage itself he judged that it was impossible to sway Habrocomes, for he saw that he was woefully disheartened in spirit, and saw too that he was in love with Anthia. He realized, furthermore, that it was inadvisable to employ force, for he feared that Habrocomes might do himself some hurt. But when they landed at Tyre he could no longer refrain himself. At first he showed Habrocomes every attention, and urged him to be of good heart, and provided him with every care. Habrocomes thought that it was because Corymbos pitied him that he was so solicitous. But then Corymbos confided his love to one of his fellow pirates, Euxinos by name; him he besought to be his aid, and to counsel him how he might persuade the lad. Euxinos was highly pleased to hear Corymbos' story, for he himself was in wretched state because of Anthia, with whom he had fallen fearfully in love. His own story, therefore, he confided to Corymbos; and advised him to suffer torment no longer, but to set at once to work. "For," said he, "an ignoble thing it were if when we have undergone peril and exposed our lives we should have no secure enjoyment of what our labors have won. We shall be able," he added, "to obtain these select items from Apsyrtos as a gift." These words easily persuaded that lover. Accordingly they agreed each to speak on the other's behalf; Euxinos would persuade Habrocomes, and Corymbos Anthia.

In the meanwhile those two were depressed in spirit; they anticipated many difficulties and spoke of them one to the other, and ever and again they swore to observe their pledges to one another. Then came to them Corymbos and Euxinos and said they wished to speak to them privately, and the one led Anthia apart, and the other Habrocomes. The hearts of these two were deeply troubled, and they expected that no good would come of it. Then Euxinos spoke to Habrocomes on Corymbos' behalf. "My lad, likely enough you feel depressed, finding yourself a slave instead of free, poor instead of rich. But you ought to charge everything up to fortune, to accommodate yourself to the lot which rules you, and to love those that have become your masters. You must know that it is possible for you to recover your wealth and your freedom if you are willing to yield to your master Corymbos. He is passionately in love with you and is ready to make you master of everything he possesses. You will undergo nothing disagreeable, but render your master more benevolent toward you. Consider the situation in which you find yourself. There is no one to help you. The country itself is alien, your masters are robbers, and there is no refuge whatever from punishment if you disdain Corymbos. What need have you now for a wife and a household? What need have you of a sweetheart at your time of life? Throw it all overboard; it is only to your master that you need to look, and to hearken to his bidding." When Habrocomes heard this he was straightway struck dumb, stupefied, and could find no answer to make; he could only weep and groan at the thought of his plight. But then he did speak to Euxinos: "Allow me, master, to deliberate a little," he said, "and I shall give you a full reply." Euxinos departed. But Corymbos spoke to Anthia of Euxinos' love, mentioning her straits and the necessity of yielding to her masters. He also made many promises if she should be persuaded—lawful matrimony, money, and abundance of all things. She too made a similar reply, requesting a short time for deliberation. Together Euxinos and Corymbos waited for the decisions, having little doubt that they could sway Habrocomes and Anthia.

2 *Habrocomes and Anthia met at their humble lodging,* and each gave the other his news. They flung themselves down and wept and wailed. "Father!" they cried. "Mother!" "Dear home!" "Family!" "Kinfolk!" Finally Habrocomes collected himself and said, "Miserable wretches that we are, what tribulations shall we undergo in this barbarous country, delivered to the brutality of pirates? The woes prophesied now begin. Now is the god exacting vengeance of me for my overweening pride. Corymbos is in love with me, Euxinos with you. Ah for our unseasonable beauty! It is for this, forsooth, that I have preserved my chastity until now, that I might submit to the filthy passion of a robber in love. What manner of life will be left for me when I have become a harlot instead of a man and have been deprived of my dear Anthia? No, by that chastity which has been my companion from childhood until now, I will *not* submit myself to Corymbos. Sooner shall I die, and as a corpse shall be proven chaste." So he said, and shed many tears. And Anthia, "Alas for our woes!" said she. "All too soon shall we be compelled

to take thought of our oaths. Soon we shall know what slavery means. A man desires me and expects to sway me and to come to my bed after Habrocomes and to lie with me and satisfy his passion. But may I never show myself so abjectly in love with life nor survive, being thus outraged, to look upon the sun. So let our determination be fixed. Let us die, Habrocomes; we shall possess one another after death and none shall trouble us."

Thus they two resolved. But in the meantime Apsyrtos, the chief of the robber band, when he learned that the party with Corymbos had returned and that the valuables they had brought were plentiful and marvelous, came to that country retreat. He observed Habrocomes and Anthia and was struck by their beauty, and, thinking he would derive large profit from them, he asked for them at once. The rest of what they had taken— money, valuables, girls—he distributed to Corymbos and his party. Euxinos and Corymbos were loath to yield Habrocomes and Anthia to Apsyrtos; yield them, however, they did. And so these two departed; but Apsyrtos took Habrocomes and Anthia, and two slaves, Leucon and Rhode, and brought them to Tyre. Their procession attracted much attention. Everyone admired their beauty, and the barbarian folk who had never before seen such comeliness thought the persons they saw were gods and felicitated Apsyrtos on the quality of the slaves he had acquired. Apsyrtos brought them to his house and turned them over to a trusted slave, whom he bade have particular care of them, for he expected large profits if he could sell them at a just price.

Such was the situation of Habrocomes and Anthia. After a few days had passed Apsyrtos departed to Syria on other business, and his daughter Manto fell in love with Habrocomes. She was pretty, and ripe for marriage, but she fell far short of Anthia's beauty. Proximity had aroused Manto's passions; she could not contain herself, and knew not what to do. To speak to Habrocomes she dared not, for she knew that he had a wife and could not hope to persuade him; nor could she speak to anyone of her people for fear of her father. Hence she burned the more ardently, and was in a wretched state. And when she could endure it no longer she determined to speak of her love to Rhode, who was Anthia's companion, her age-fellow and a girl. In her alone she hoped to find one who would assist her in her passion. Seizing then on a suitable opportunity, she took the girl to the ancestral chapel in her house and implored her not to betray her and exacted an oath, and then told of her love for Habrocomes and besought her to take her part and made large promises if she would. Said she, "Know you that you are my slave, know too that you will feel my fury, a barbarian's fury, if you do me hurt." When she had said so much she dismissed Rhode, who now found herself at an impasse. To speak to Habrocomes she abhorred, for she loved Anthia; but she dreaded the fury of the barbarian. And so she decided to tell Leucon what she had heard from Manto. Between Rhode and Leucon there was a lovers' understanding; they had been intimate even in Ephesus. Finding him alone, then, Rhode said, "We are utterly lost, Leucon; no longer shall we have our companions. The daughter of our master Apsyrtos has conceived an ardent love for Habrocomes and threatens to do us grievous hurt if she does not obtain her desire. See, then, what we have to do. To refuse a barbarian woman is a dangerous thing, to separate Habrocomes from Anthia an impossible one." When Leucon heard this he burst into tears, foreseeing great evils to come. But then he collected himself and said, "Silence, Rhode! I shall manage the whole matter."

When he had so said he went to Habrocomes. Habrocomes had no other concern than to love Anthia and to be loved by her, to talk with her and to hear her talk. Leucon approached them and said, "What are we to do, comrades? How shall we plan, fellow slaves? One of our masters, Habrocomes, finds you beautiful. The daughter of Apsyrtos is in a desperate state about you, and it is a hard thing to reject a barbarian girl in love. Be advised then as seems to you best, but save us all and do not look idly on when we are about to succumb to the fury of our masters." When Habrocomes heard this he was incensed. He glared at Leucon and said, "You scoundrel, more barbarous than the Phoenicians here, have you dared to utter such words to Habrocomes, to mention another girl when Anthia is present? A slave I am, indeed, but I know how to keep engagements. They may have power over my body, but my soul I keep free. Let Manto now threaten swords, if she will, and nooses and fire and all the tortures that can force the body of a slave: never shall I be persuaded willingly to deal unfairly with Anthia." This is what Habrocomes said, but Anthia was stupefied by the disaster and could not utter a word. Finally and with difficulty she roused herself, and she said, "I possess your heart, and I believe that I am most singularly loved by you. But I beg of you, who are master of my soul, do not betray yourself nor deliver yourself to a barbarian's fury; submit to the passion of your mistress. I shall go off somewhere and kill myself. So much I ask of you: bury me yourself, and kiss me when I have fallen, and remember Anthia." All of this plunged Habrocomes into even greater distress; he knew not what to expect. Such then was the situation in which they found themselves.

Manto, when Rhode delayed in returning, could no longer master herself, but wrote a letter to Habrocomes, in words as follows:

To Habrocomes the fair: thy mistress salutes thee.

Manto loves thee, and can no longer endure. Unseemly perhaps my conduct is for a maiden, but, for one who loves, necessary. I implore thee, do not scorn me, and do not affront one who has thy interests at heart. If thou hearken to me, I will persuade my father Apsyrtos to marry me to thee; we shall get rid of thy present wife, and thou wilt be rich and blessed. But if thou refuse, consider what pains thou wilt suffer when she that is affronted wreaks her vengeance, and what pains await thine associates who have proven themselves counselors to thine arrogance.

This letter she took and sealed, and gave it to one of her own servants, a barbarian woman, and bade her deliver it to Habrocomes. He received it and read it, and was sore troubled by all it said, but chiefly he was distressed by the threat to Anthia. That tablet he retained, and he wrote another and gave it to the handmaiden, of which the words were the following:

Mistress, do what thou wilt, use my body as a slave's. If thy wish is to slay me, I am ready; if to torture me, torture as thou wilt. To thy bed I shall not come, nor should I obey in such matters even if thou command me.

When Manto received this letter she fell into fury unrestrained, compounded of all passions—envy and jealousy and pain and fear; and she planned dire punishment for the man who disdained her.

At this conjuncture Apsyrtos returned from Syria, bringing with him a young man named Moeris as a groom for his daughter. When he arrived Manto straightway staged her plot against Habrocomes. She pulled her hair apart, tore her robe in tatters, went to meet her father, fell at his knees, and cried, "Take pity, Father, upon your daughter who has been outrageously entreated by a slave. That virtuous Habrocomes has made an attempt upon my maidenhood and so has betrayed you too, saying that he was in love with me. Punish him as his infamous boldness deserves. But if you do consent to give your own daughter to slaves, I will prevent you by killing myself."

When Apsyrtos heard this he thought she spoke truth and took no thought to inquire into the matter. He summoned Habrocomes and said to him, "Creature vile and accursed, have you dared to outrage your own masters and have you sought to corrupt a maiden, yourself a slave? But you will take no pleasure from your conduct. I will punish you, I will make your horrible suffering an example for other slaves." He spoke, and, impatient and unwilling to listen, he ordered his slaves to rip Habrocomes' garments off, to bring fire and whips, and to scourge the lad. Pitiful indeed was the spectacle. The torments disfigured that whole body, which was unused to slave punishments, the blood flowed down, and his beauty faded away. They brought fearful chains and applied fire and used excruciating torments upon him—to demonstrate to his daughter's bridegroom that he would marry a virtuous maiden. In the meanwhile Anthia fell at Apsyrotos' knees and implored him on Habrocomes' behalf. But he said, "Nay, rather shall he be more cruelly tortured for your sake, for you too had he injured, loving another though he had you to wife." Then he bade them bind him in chains and incarcerate him in a dark dungeon.

Now was Habrocomes fettered and cast into prison; dark despair seized upon him, and especially when he saw no Anthia. He tried many methods of inducing death, but could find none, for those who guarded him were many. But Apsyrtos celebrated the marriage of his daughter and kept festival for many days. Anthia for her part was a mass of grief. Whenever she was able to cajole the jailers she entered in to Habrocomes secretly and lamented their catastrophe. And when the bridal company were now preparing to depart to Syria, Apsyrtos escorted his daughter with many gifts, and he presented her with Babylonian fabrics and boundless silver and gold. To his daughter Manto he presented also Anthia and Rhode and Leucon. When Anthia learned of this and knew that she would be carried to Syria with Manto, she contrived to enter the prison, and embraced Habrocomes, and said to him, "My lord, I am being taken to Syria, given as a gift to Manto; I am delivered into the hands of that jealous woman. You will remain in the prison and die pitifully, and you will have no one to care for your body. But I swear to you by the power that controls us both that I will remain yours, whether I live or whether I needs must die." So saying, she kissed him and embraced him and caressed his chains and writhed at his feet.

At length she departed out of the prison. But he, just as he was, flung himself upon the ground and wept, saying, "O my dearest Father, O Themiste my Mother! Where now is that happiness that once distinguished us in Ephesus? Where are the brilliant and famous Anthia and Habrocomes, those admired beauties? She has gone to the far ends of the earth as a captive, and I now am deprived of my sole solace and shall wretchedly die in prison and alone." When he said this sleep overtook him and there appeared to him a dream. He thought he saw his own father, Lycomedes, clothed in black, wandering over every land and sea, and finally arriving at the prison, freeing him and releasing him from the dungeon. Himself he saw then transformed to a horse and galloping over much territory in pursuit of another who was a mare; finally he found the mare and recovered his human shape. After he saw this dream he rose up, and was somewhat more hopeful.

But Habrocomes remained immured in the prison and Anthia was taken to Syria, along with Leucon and Rhode. When those in Manto's party reached Antioch (which was Moeris' country), she dealt maliciously with Rhode, and hated Anthia bitterly. She gave orders at once that Rhode and Leucon should be loaded on a ship and sold in some place remote from the Syrian country. Anthia she planned to join to a slave, and at that to the vilest sort, a rustic goatherd; this she thought a suitable vengeance. And so she summoned the goatherd, whose name was Lampo, and delivered Anthia to his hands and bade him take her to wife, and she ordered him to use force if Anthia should be unwilling. Anthia was carried off to the country to cohabit with the goatherd. But when she arrived where Lampo kept his goats she fell at his knees and begged him to pity her and preserve her chastity. She explained who she was, and told of her high birth, her husband, her captivity. When Lampo heard these things he took pity upon the girl and swore that he would verily keep her chaste and bade her take heart.

And so Anthia lived at the goatherd's in the country, lamenting Habrocomes all the while. Apsyrtos, rummaging through the cubicle where Habrocomes had lived before his punishment, came upon Manto's letter to Habrocomes. He recognized the writing, and realized that Habrocomes had been unjustly punished. He ordered that he be loosed forthwith and brought into his presence. Though he had been so disgracefully and cruelly treated, Habrocomes fell at his knees; but Apsyrtos raised him up and said, "Take heart, my boy; unjustly did I condemn you, being persuaded by my daughter's words. But now I will make you a free man instead of a slave. I will put you in charge of the management of my house, and I will procure the daughter of one of my fellow citizens to be your wife. Do not cherish evil thoughts for what has happened; it was not of my own will that I did you injury." These were the words of Apsyrtos, but Habrocomes said, "I thank you, master, for learning the truth and for recompensing my virtue." Everyone in the whole household was delighted for Habrocomes' sake, and they thanked the master on his behalf. But he himself was in deep distress because of Anthia, and frequently did he reflect to himself: "What good is freedom to me? What good is wealth and the management of Apsyrtos' affairs? That is not the sort of man I want to be. It is that girl that I would wish to find, whether she be alive or dead." Such, then, was Habrocomes' situation. He managed Apsyrtos' affairs, indeed, but he kept thinking when and where he might find Anthia. Now Leucon and Rhode had been carried to Xanthos, a city in Lycia, not far from the sea, and there they were sold to a certain old man who treated them with great consideration; he regarded them as his own children, for he was himself childless. They passed their time in ease and plenty, but were grieved because they no longer saw Anthia and Habrocomes.

Now Anthia lived for some time at the goatherd's; but Moeris, Manto's husband, who visited that country place frequently, conceived a passion for Anthia. At first he tried to dissemble his love, but finally he spoke to the goatherd and made him lavish promises if he would lend him his efforts. For his part the goatherd agreed to Moeris' proposal, but he feared Manto, and so went to her and informed her of Moeris' love. She then fell into a rage and said, "Most unfortunate of all women am I. My own rival I carry with me; through her at first in Phoenicia I was deprived of my love, and now I risk losing my husband to her. But Anthia will find no pleasure in having attracted Moeris too by her beauty. Here my vengeance shall be harsher than in Tyre." For the time being Manto kept her peace, but when Moeris was away on a journey she summoned the goatherd and ordered him to seize Anthia, carry her into the thickest part of the forest, and there kill her; for this service she promised to pay him well.

The goatherd took pity on the girl, indeed, but dreaded Manto; so he came to Anthia and told her all that had been decreed against her. She cried out and lamented, saying, "Alas, everywhere that fatal beauty proves a snare for both of us. Because of that beauty Habrocomes has died in Tyre, and I die here. But I pray you, dear goatherd Lampo, deal piously with me as you have done heretofore. If you kill me give me burial, however humble, in the earth nearby, and place your hands over my eyes, and as you bury me call the name of Habrocomes repeatedly. Such a burial would be for me the happiest." So she spoke, and the goatherd took pity upon her. He reflected that he would be perpetrating an infamous crime in killing a girl who was guilty of no wrong, and one so fair. Though he laid hold of the girl, he could not endure to kill her. Instead he said to her, "Anthia, you know that my mistress, Manto, has ordered me to seize and murder you. But I fear the gods and have pity for your beauty, and so I choose rather to sell you far away from this country, so that Manto may not learn that you have not died and so will not hurt me." At this Anthia wept and clasped his feet and said, "May the gods and our ancestral deity, Artemis, render the goatherd due requital for his benefactions!" She urged him then to sell her. And so the goatherd took Anthia and went to the harbor. There he found Cilician merchants, to whom he sold the girl, and when he had received her price he returned to his fields. The merchants took Anthia and embarked her upon a boat, and as night came on they sailed for Cilicia. But they were caught by contrary winds, and upon the ship breaking up only few were able to reach shore by clinging to planks; these had Anthia with them. Where they landed was a dense forest, in which they wandered through the night; later they were taken captive by the brigand Hippothoos and his band.

In the meanwhile there arrived from Syria a slave bringing a letter from Manto to her father, Apsyrtos, in the words following:

> You gave me to a husband in a foreign land. Anthia, whom you presented to me along with other slaves, worked much evil against me, and I ordered her to live in a rural district. My handsome Moeris, who saw her constantly in that country place, fell in love with her. When I could no longer tolerate this situation I summoned the goatherd and bade him sell the girl again in some city of Syria.

When Habrocomes learned of this he could no longer find the heart to stay; eluding Apsyrtos and all the rest of the household, he went forth in search of Anthia. Presently he reached

the countryside where Anthia had passed her days with the goatherd. He encountered that same goatherd, Lampo, to whom
Manto had given Anthia to wife, and begged him to tell whether
he had any knowledge of a girl from Tyre. The goatherd told
him of a Tyrian girl, named Anthia, and recounted the rest—
the marriage, his pious conduct toward her, the love of Moeris,
the decree against her, and the journey to Cilicia. He said, too,
that the girl was always speaking of one Habrocomes. Habrocomes himself did not reveal his identity, but he rose early in
the morning and took horse for Cilicia, hoping to find Anthia
there.

That first night, in the meanwhile, Hippothoos and his robber band spent in feasting, and on the following day they busied
themselves with sacrifice. Everything was got ready—the image
of Ares, wood, and garlands—and the sacrifice was due to take
place in the customary fashion. Whatever victim they were going to sacrifice, whether it were human or animal, they would
hang from a tree and then take position at a distance and aim
their javelins at it; when they hit the mark they thought the
sacrifice was acceptable to the god, and when they missed it they
would renew their offerings to gain Ares' favor. For this service
of sacrifice Anthia was the chosen victim. When everything was
now ready and they were about to hang the girl, a crashing was
heard in the forest and the beat of marching men. This was
the chief of law and order in Cilicia, Perilaos by name, one of
the principal personages in Cilicia. This Perilaos attacked the
brigands with a large force, and dispatched them all, taking a
few alive as captives. Only Hippothoos was able to escape and
take his weapons with him. Anthia came into the hands of
Perilaos, and when he learned of the ordeal she had been about
to undergo he took pity upon her. But that pity was the beginning of great woe for Anthia. Her and those robbers whom he
had made prisoner he took to Tarsus in Cilicia. Proximity and
the frequent sight of the girl led him on the path of love, and
little by little Perilaos was wholly captivated by Anthia. When
they arrived at Tarsus, the brigands he delivered to imprisonment, but to Anthia he paid steady court. Neither wife nor
children had Perilaos, and the sum of his possessions was by no

means inconsiderable; and so he urged upon Anthia that she would be all in all to him—wife and chatelaine and children. At first Anthia refused, but since she had no means of rejecting his vehemence and his great persistence, and feared lest he might grow so bold as to use violence, she finally agreed, indeed, to the marriage, but pleaded with him to wait for a short period, as much as thirty days, and to keep her untouched in the interval, alleging some pretext or other for her request. Perilaos agreed and swore he would preserve her untouched until the stated period should elapse.

And so Anthia remained in Tarsus with Perilaos, awaiting the season of her marriage. Now Habrocomes proceeded on his road to Cilicia. Not far from the cave of the brigands (he had wandered from the straight road) he encountered Hippothoos, who was fully armed. When the latter saw him he ran to meet him and greeted him in friendly wise and invited him to share the road with him. "Whoever you may be, my boy," said he, "I see that you are handsome to look at and have a manly bearing. Your wandering about indicates that you have somehow been wronged. Let us leave Cilicia behind, then, and go to Cappadocia and to Pontus; those that live there, they say, are happy." Habrocomes said nothing of his search for Anthia, but he agreed to the proposal of Hippothoos, who was insistent, and they swore to render one another co-operation and assistance. It was Habrocomes' hope that in the course of much wandering he might find Anthia. For that day, then, they returned to the cave, to spend as much of it as was left in refreshing themselves and their horses. For Hippothoos, too, had a horse, which he kept concealed in the forest.

3 *On the next day they left Cilicia and made their way* toward Mazacos, a large and beautiful city in Cappadocia. There Hippothoos had it in mind to recruit a body of rugged young men and to reconstitute his robber band. As they proceeded through large villages they found a great abundance of all necessaries. Hippothoos was familiar with the Cappadocian language, and everyone treated him like a native. After ten days of travel they arrived at Mazacos; there they found lodging near the city gates, and they resolved to spend some days in refreshing themselves from the laborious journey. It chanced as they were feasting that Hippothoos fetched a deep sigh and began to weep. Habrocomes inquired what the cause of his tears might be. "Mine is a long history," said Hippothoos, "and one rich in tragedy." Habrocomes begged him to speak, and promised that he would recount his own history in turn. They happened to be alone, and so Hippothoos, beginning his tale at the beginning, related the following narrative of his life:

"By birth I belong to the city of Perinthos, which lies near Thrace, and my family is among the most distinguished in that place. You have surely heard tell how celebrated a city Perinthos is, and how happy its inhabitants are. In Perinthos, when I was still young, I fell in love with a lad; he was a native boy, and his name was Hyperanthes. My love first began when I saw him wrestling in the gymnasium, and I could not contain myself. When a local festival that included all-night vigils was being celebrated, I approached Hyperanthes and implored him to take pity on me; and when the lad heard all my story he promised to show me compassion. The first stages of love were kisses and fondlings and (on my part) abundant tears. Finally we seized an opportunity to be alone together; our equal age obviated suspicion.

"For a long time we were together and loved one another passionately, until some deity begrudged us. There came from Byzantium (Byzantium is near Perinthos) a certain man who held great influence there; he was proud and rich, and he was called Aristomachos. As soon as this man set foot in Perinthos— as if some deity had specifically sent him to my bane—he caught sight of Hyperanthes and was straightway smitten; he admired the lad's beauty—which was indeed enough to allure anyone. And, having fallen in love, he could not keep his passion within moderation, but immediately sent proposals to the boy. When this proved futile (for Hyperanthes would admit no one because of his affection for me) he persuaded the lad's father, who was a vile creature with a weakness for money. The father delivered Hyperanthes over to the man on the pretext of education, for he was an accomplished rhetorician. So the man took him, and at first kept him shut up fast, and afterwards went off to Byzantium with him. I abandoned all my own concerns and followed, and on every possible occasion I was in the lad's company; but the occasions were few indeed; a rare kiss fell to my lot, a snatch of difficult conversation—there were too many people to keep watch.

"Finally, when I could endure it no longer, I roused myself to action; I returned to Perinthos, sold everything I possessed, and with the moneys I collected I went to Byzantium. I took a dagger (this had been agreed to by Hyperanthes), entered Aristomachos' house at night, and found him lying beside the boy; filled with fury, I struck Aristomachos a fatal blow. It was quiet and everyone was asleep, and I departed as secretly as I had come, taking Hyperanthes with me. All that night we made our way to Perinthos, and at once, none being privy, we went aboard ship and sailed for Asia. Up to a point our voyage prospered well, but presently, when we were near Lesbos, a mighty gale struck us and overturned our vessel. I swam along with Hyperanthes, supporting him and making his swimming lighter; but when night came the boy could no longer sustain the effort and gave over swimming and so died. I did what I could to get the body safe to land and bury it. Much did I weep and groan, and I collected the remains; and when I succeeded in securing a suitable stone I set up a marker on the grave, and as a memorial of the unfortunate lad I inscribed upon it an epitaph which I composed on the spur of the moment:

This monument hath Hippothoos fashioned for famous Hyperanthes,
Not worthy of a sacred citizen deceased,
A famous flower, whom on a time from land to the deep a deity
Ravished in the sea, when a stiff gale blew.

"Thereafter I determined not to return to Perinthos, and directed my footsteps through Asia to great Phrygia and Pamphylia. There, for want of livelihood and in discouragement at my lot, I devoted myself to brigandage. At first I became an underling in a robber band, but eventually I myself set up such a band in Cilicia. I achieved a great reputation, until, shortly before I caught sight of you, the men of my company were taken prisoner. Such then is the narrative of my fortunes. And now do you, dear friend, tell me your story, for it is plainly by reason of some great compulsion that you lead a vagabond existence."

Habrocomes said that he was of Ephesus, that he fell in love with a girl and had married her, and then he told of the oracles, the voyage abroad, the pirates, Apsyrtos, Manto, the imprisonment, the escape, the goatherd, and the journey to Cilicia. While he was yet speaking Hippothoos joined in his lamentations, saying, "O my parents, O my country which I shall nevermore behold, O Hyperanthes dearer to me than all! You, Habrocomes, will see your beloved, and someday will recover her; but I can never see Hyperanthes again." As he spoke he showed a lock of his beloved's hair, and wept over it. Now when they had both had their fill of sorrow Hippothoos looked at Habrocomes and said, "One episode I omitted in my narrative. A little before the robber band was made prisoner, there arrived at our cave a beautiful girl who had lost her way. She was of the same age as yours, and mentioned your home city as her fatherland; I learned nothing more about her. We decided to sacrifice her to Ares, and all was in readiness when our pursuers launched their attack. I myself escaped; what became of her I do not know. She was very beautiful, Habrocomes; she was simply dressed, her hair was yellow, her eyes charming." While he was yet speaking Habrocomes cried out, "It is my Anthia that you have seen, Hippothoos! Whither can she have fled? What country holds her now? To Cilicia let us return, and there search for her; she cannot be far from the robbers' cave. Verily, by the soul of Hyperanthes, I implore you, do not willfully wrong me, but let us go where we shall be able to find Anthia!" Hippothoos promised to do all in his power, but declared that it was essential for them to enlist a few men for the sake of safety on the road.

This, then, was their situation, and they pondered how they might best make their way back to Cilicia. But for Anthia the thirty days had now passed, and preparations were on foot for her marriage to Perilaos. Sacrificial animals had been brought in from the country, and there was a great abundance of other things. All his relatives and friends had gathered together to share in the festivities and many of his fellow citizens joined in the celebration for Anthia's marriage.

At the time when Anthia was rescued from the robber band there came to Tarsus an elderly Ephesian, Eudoxos by name and a physician by profession; sailing toward Egypt, his ship had been wrecked near the Cilician shore. This Eudoxos went about soliciting all the gentry of Tarsus, asking some for clothing and others for money, and recounting his misfortunes to each. He approached Perilaos also, and told him that he was an Ephesian and a physician by profession. Perilaos took him up, and brought him to Anthia, thinking that she would be overjoyed to see a man from Ephesus. She gave Eudoxos a friendly welcome, and inquired whether he had any news to tell of her own people. He said that he had been long absent from Ephesus and so had no tidings; nonetheless Anthia took pleasure in his society, for it brought to her mind memories of people at home. And thus Eudoxos became a familiar of the household and frequently addressed himself to Anthia; he enjoyed all the resources of the house, but always besought her to have him sent back to Ephesus, for he had a wife and children in that city.

Now when all preparations had been completed for the marriage of Perilaos and the day was at hand, a sumptuous feast was prepared for them and Anthia was decked out in bridal array. But neither by night nor by day had she surcease of tears; always she had Habrocomes before her eyes. Many thoughts coursed through her mind—her love, her oaths, her country, her parents, her constraint, her marriage. And when she found herself alone she seized the occasion and tore her hair and said, "Ah, wholly unjust am I and wicked, for I do not requite Habrocomes' loyalty to me. To remain my husband, he endured fetters and torture, and now may somewhere lie dead; but I am oblivious to all these things, and am being married, wretch that I am, and someone will chant the hymeneal over me and I shall go to the bed of Perilaos. But ah, Habrocomes, dearest soul of all, do not afflict yourself over me; never willingly would I wrong you.

I come to join you, and until death will remain your bride."

Thus she said, and when Eudoxos, the Ephesian physician, came to her, she led him aside to a certain vacant chamber, and fell at his knees and petitioned him not to reveal anything she would say to anyone, and exacted an oath by their ancestral deity, Artemis, that he would help her in whatever way she would request. Eudoxos raised her up as she wailed disconsolately, and bade her take heart, and promised upon oath that he would do everything. She told him then of her love for Habrocomes, of the oaths she had sworn to him, and of their engagements in regard to chastity. And then she said, "If it were possible for me, being alive, to recover Habrocomes alive, or else to flee from this place in secret, I should take counsel for such courses. But since Habrocomes is dead and it is impractical for me to escape and impossible to abide the approaching marriage—for I will neither transgress my pledges to Habrocomes nor will I despise an oath—do you then be my helper; find me somewhere a drug which will release wretched me from my tribulations. In return for this service you will receive much recompense from the gods, whom I shall ardently and frequently beseech on your behalf before my death, and I myself will give you money and arrange your return to Ephesus. Before anyone discovers anything that has transpired, you will be able to take ship and sail to Ephesus. And when you arrive there inquire for my parents, Megamedes and Evippe, and give them a report of my death and all that happened on my travels; say, too, that Habrocomes has perished."

When she had so spoken she writhed at his feet and implored him not to refuse to give her the poison. Then she produced twenty minae of silver and her necklaces (all things she had in abundance, for all Perilaos' property was at her disposal) and gave them to Eudoxos. He deliberated for a long while: he pitied the girl for her misfortunes, he yearned to return to Ephesus, he coveted the money and the jewels; and so he promised to give her the drug, and went off to fetch it. She, in the meantime, was sunk in grief. She lamented her youth and was anguished at the thought of her untimely death; and frequently she called upon Habrocomes as though he were present. After no long while

Eudoxos arrived bringing a drug, not lethal, however, but only hypnotic, so that no real harm should come to the girl and he himself meanwhile make arrangements for travel and be on his way. Anthia received the potion, thanked him warmly, and dismissed him. He then took ship and sailed away, and Anthia awaited a suitable moment for imbibing the poison.

Now was night fallen, and the bridal chamber was made ready, and those charged with the duty came to lead Anthia forth. She did go forth, all unwilling and suffused with tears, and she held the drug hidden in her hand. When she drew near the bridal chamber the members of the household chanted the propitious hymeneal, but Anthia grieved and wept, saying, "Just so, upon a time, was I led to my bridegroom, Habrocomes, and the torches of love escorted us, and the hymeneal was sung for our propitious union. And now what will you do, Anthia? Will you wrong Habrocomes, your husband, who loves you, who has died because of you? Nay, I am not so cowardly nor have my misfortunes made me so fearful. It is resolved: I shall drink the drug. Habrocomes must be my only husband; him do I desire though he is dead." This she said, and she was conducted in to the bridal chamber.

And now she found herself alone, for Perilaos was still feasting with his friends. She pretended that the agitation had made her thirsty, and bade one of the servants to bring her water to drink. And when the cup was brought, she took it, when no one was by, and cast the drug into it, and she wept, saying, "Ah, dearest soul, Habrocomes, lo, I discharge my promises to you, and I embark upon my journey to you, an unhappy journey but an inevitable one. Receive me gladly, and make my sojourn there with you a happy one." When she had so spoken she drank up the drug. Immediately sleep held her fast and she fell to the ground; the drug had accomplished its full task.

When Perilaos entered the chamber, as soon as he caught sight of Anthia lying unconscious, he was stunned and cried out. There was a great tumult among the whole household, and mingled emotions—lamentations and horror and stupefaction. Some were moved by pity for the girl seemingly dead, others sympathized with Perilaos' affliction, all bewailed what had happened. Perilaos rent his garments and threw himself upon the body, saying, "Ah, my dearest girl: before your marriage, alas, you have left your lover behind, his destined bride of but a few days. . . . Is it the tomb to which we shall bring you as a bridal chamber? Happy indeed that Habrocomes, whoever he was, truly blessed is he, receiving such a gift from his beloved." So he lamented, and he held all her body close, and caressed her hands and feet saying, "My poor bride, my more unhappy wife." Then he adorned her, wrapping rich robes about her body and decking it with much gold. The sight of her was too much for his endurance, and when day dawned he placed Anthia (who lay unconscious) upon a bier and conveyed her to the cemetery near the city. There he deposited her in a funerary chamber, having immolated many victims and consumed many garments and other attire in flames.

When he had completed the customary rites Perilaos was conducted back to the city by his household. Anthia, who had been left in the tomb, recovered her consciousness, and when she realized that the potion had not been lethal she groaned and wept, saying, "Ah, drug that has deceived me, that has prevented me from pursuing my happy journey to Habrocomes. Wholly hapless as I am, I am balked even in my yearning for death. But it is yet possible for me to remain in this tomb and by starvation bring the work of the drug to accomplishment. From here none shall remove me, nor would I look upon the sun, nor shall I rise to the light of day." Thus saying she made her heart firm and awaited death with fortitude.

In the meanwhile certain robbers had learned that the girl had received a rich burial, that much female finery had been deposited with her, and a large quantity of silver and gold; when night fell they approached the tomb and broke through the doors of the vault and entered it. They laid hands on the valuables, and beheld Anthia alive. They reckoned that this too would be a great profit, so they raised the girl up and wished to carry her off. But she humbled herself at their feet and petitioned them earnestly, saying, "Sirs, whoever you may be, all this attire, as much as there is, and all the things buried with me here, take and carry off; but spare my person. I am consecrated to two deities, Love and Death: leave me free for my devotion to them. I pray you, in the name of your own ancestral gods, do not show to the light of day one whose misfortunes deserve night and darkness." Thus she spoke, but could not persuade the robbers. They brought her out of the tomb and conducted her down to the sea and placed her upon a boat, upon which they sailed for Alexandria. On the vessel they tended her well and bade her take heart. But she reflected upon the evils into which she was again fallen, and lamented and moaned, saying, "Again brigands and the sea, again am I a captive. But now I am the more wretched, for I am not with Habrocomes. What country will now receive me? What manner of men shall I see? Never, I pray, a Moeris, never Manto, never Perilaos, never Cilicia. But may I come where I might at least see the tomb of Habrocomes!" Whenever she thought upon these things she wept. She herself would take no drink and no sustenance, but the robbers compelled her to do so. They prosecuted their voyage, and after many days' sailing arrived at Alexandria. There they disembarked Anthia, and resolved to sell her to certain merchants forthwith.

Perilaos for his part learned that the tomb had been broken open and the body spirited away, and suffered affliction great and intolerable. Now Habrocomes pursued his search and busily inquired whether anyone had any knowledge of a foreign girl who had been taken captive by robbers and carried off. When he could discover nothing he was wearied and returned where they lodged. Those with Hippothoos had prepared a meal for them, and the others, too, dined with them. But Habrocomes was low in spirits and threw himself upon the couch and wept; there he lay, and would take no food. As those in Hippothoos' company proceeded with their drinking a certain old woman there present, named Chrysion, began to tell a story. "Listen, friends," said she, "to a tale of a thing that lately happened in the city. A man called Perilaos, one of the important people here, was elected chief of law and order in Cilicia, and went out to search for brigands. He did arrest some robbers and brought them in, and with them was a beautiful girl; her he persuaded to marry him. All the preparations for the wedding were completed, and the girl entered the bridal chamber. Then, whether she had gone mad or because she was in love with some other she drank poison she had somehow procured, and died. So the manner of her death was described."

When Hippothoos heard this he said, "That is the very girl for whom Habrocomes is searching." Habrocomes too had heard the tale, but had let it pass because he was so dispirited. But at the sound of Hippothoos' voice he finally, and with difficulty, aroused himself and said: "Now of a certainty is Anthia dead; but perhaps her grave is here and her body is safe." So saying, he besought the old woman, Chrysion, to conduct him to Anthia's tomb and show him the body. But she fetched a deep sigh and said, "Now comes the most unfortunate thing of all that has befallen that unhappy girl. For his part Perilaos buried her sumptuously and provided ornaments; but robbers who learned of the valuables buried with her broke open the tomb and carried off the ornaments and spirited the body away. Perilaos has instituted an intense investigation into the affair." When Habrocomes heard this he tore his tunic to tatters and wailed loudly for Anthia, who had so nobly and chastely died, but who had so unhappily perished after her death. "What robber," he cried, "is so passionate a lover as to lust even for your corpse and snatch your dead body away? Wretch that I am, I am deprived even of your remains, my only solace. Now am I altogether determined to die; but first I must endure until I find your body, and when I have embraced it I shall bury myself along with it." So he said in his grief; but Hippothoos and his company bade him take heart. Then they went to their rest for all that night.

But the mind of Habrocomes was invaded by many thoughts —of Anthia, of her death, of her burial, of her loss. And then, when he could no longer endure it, without attracting notice (drink had put Hippothoos and his friends into a deep sleep) he went out as if to satisfy some need, and made his way down to the sea. There he came upon a boat about to depart for Alexandria; upon this he embarked and sailed, hoping that he might overtake in Egypt the robbers who had plundered and ravaged all. In this course his guide was the hope of despair. And so Habrocomes sailed to Alexandria. In the morning Hip-

pothoos and his friends were chagrined at his departure, but
when they had taken a few days to refresh themselves they determined to proceed toward Syria and Phoenicia to engage in
brigandage.

Now the robbers had sold Anthia to merchants in Alexandria
and had received a high price for her. These merchants fed her
lavishly and tended her person, being always on the lookout for
a purchaser who would pay a just price. There had come to
Alexandria from India a prince of that country for the purpose
of seeing the sights of the city and of transacting business; his
name was Psammis. This Psammis saw Anthia in the merchants'
establishment and was much taken with the sight: he paid the
merchants their high price, and took the girl to be his hand-
maid. No sooner had that barbarian fellow bought her than he
attempted to force her in order to satisfy his desires. Anthia was
unwilling and at first refused; then she pretended to Psammis
(your barbarian is superstitious by nature) that at her birth
her father had consecrated her to Isis until the season of her
marriage, and she declared that the period had still a year to
run. "If you commit an outrage upon a maiden dedicated to the
goddess," she added, "the goddess will grow angry and her
punishment will be hard." Psammis was persuaded by the story;
he prostrated himself to the goddess and abstained from Anthia.

And so Anthia was under watch in the house of Psammis, and
supposed to be consecrated to Isis. But the ship which carried
Habrocomes missed the course to Alexandria and was cast up
near the mouth of the Nile called Paralion, by the shores of
Phoenicia. As the crew came tumbling out of their ship they
were overrun by shepherds of the region. These plundered their
cargo and threw the men into chains, and then brought them
by a long desert trail to Pelusium, a city of Egypt; there they
sold one to one purchaser and another to another. Habrocomes
was purchased by a veteran soldier who was retired, named
Araxos. This Araxos had a wife who was ugly to look at but much
worse to listen to; her intemperance passed imagination, and her
name was Bitch. Bitch conceived a passion for Habrocomes as
soon as he was brought into the house; nor could she at all refrain herself, but was terrible in her love and terrible in her

desire to give play to her passion. Araxos for his part was fond of Habrocomes and treated him as a son; but Bitch spoke to him only of sex and begged him to consent and promised to take him for a husband and to kill Araxos. To Habrocomes this seemed monstrous, and at the same time he thought much of Anthia, of the oaths, and of the chastity which had already cost him much woe. But finally he assented to Bitch's insistence. When night came Bitch killed Araxos, with a view to having Habrocomes as her husband, and she told Habrocomes what she had done. But Habrocomes could not tolerate so uninhibited a woman, and so he departed from the house and left her behind, declaring that he could never lie beside so foul a murderess. But Bitch collected herself, and at daybreak went to where the populace of Pelusium congregated; there she bewailed her husband and said that a newly bought slave had murdered him. She lamented long and loud, and the multitude believed that she spoke the truth. Immediately they arrested Habrocomes, and then sent him in chains to the then governor of Egypt. And so Habrocomes was taken to Alexandria to pay the penalty for his alleged murder of his master, Araxos.

4 *Now Hippothoos and his company moved from* Tarsus and proceeded toward Syria, making themselves master of everything that came in their way. Villages they burned, and they massacred many people. Sweeping on in this manner, they arrived at Laodicea in Syria, and there they sojourned, not, however, as robbers, but as if they had come to see the sights of the city. There Hippothoos particularly busied himself to see whether he could find Habrocomes, but his efforts were futile. And so the men refreshed themselves, and then turned to the road toward Phoenicia, and thence toward Egypt, for they had decided to overrun Egypt. When they had assembled a large band of robbers they marched toward Pelusium, then sailed the river Nile to Egyptian Hermopolis and Schedia. Then they entered the canal of the river constructed under Menelaos, and

so by-passed Alexandria but reached Memphis, the sacred city of Isis, and then Mende. From the natives, too, they recruited men to share their robber life and to serve them as guides of the way. They passed through Taua and arrived at Leontopolis, and then passed not a few other villages, of which the greater number were undistinguished [*emended text:* "they extinguished"] and arrived at Coptos, which is near Ethiopia. There they decided to set up their practice of brigandage, for the route was much frequented by merchants who traveled regularly to Ethiopia or to India. Moreover their band now amounted to five hundred men; and so when they had seized the heights on the Ethiopian side and had put their caves in order, they resolved to plunder those that traveled past.

The people of Pelusium had sent to the ruler of Egypt an account of what had happened there—that Araxos had been murdered and that it was a slave who had dared perpetrate the deed. When Habrocomes came to him, therefore, he knew all the details, and, not troubling to make inquiries concerning what had in fact taken place, he ordered the men who had brought Habrocomes to fix him to a cross. His many troubles had made Habrocomes lethargic, and he consoled himself for his imminent death by the thought that Anthia too had died. Those to whom the task was assigned brought him to the banks of the Nile where a sheer cliff looked out upon the channel of the river. There they set up their cross and attached him to it, making his hands and feet fast with ropes; for such was the procedure in crucifixion among the people of that region. Then they left him and departed, for the man crucified was secure.

But Habrocomes turned his eyes to the sun, and then looked upon the stream of the Nile, and said, "O thou of gods most benevolent to man, who dost hold Egypt in thy sway and hast made earth and sea appear to all mankind: if Habrocomes has committed any wrong, may I perish miserably and undergo even crueller punshiment than this, if such there be; but if I have been betrayed by a lewd woman, may the stream of Nile never be polluted by the body of a man unjustly done to death, and may you never look upon the spectacle of a man innocent of any wrong perishing here in thy land." So he prayed, and the god had compassion upon him. Suddenly a gust of wind arose and smote the cross and crumbled the earth of the cliff upon which the cross was fixed. Habrocomes fell into the stream and was borne along, and neither did the water injure him nor his bonds impede him nor wild beasts do him hurt; but the flood was his escort, and he was borne along until he reached the mouth of the Nile, where it empties into the sea. There those who were posted as guards seized him and brought him to the administrator of Egypt as a fugitive from punishment.

The governor was even more deeply incensed and thought this a consummate wickedness; he therefore ordered his men to erect a pyre, place Habrocomes upon it, and consume him in flames. And now all was made ready: the pyre was built at the mouth of the Nile, Habrocomes was placed upon it, the pyre was kindled. But just as the flame was on the point of enveloping his body, Habrocomes again prayed briefly, as best he was able, that he be saved from instant destruction. Then did the Nile rise in waves and its stream poured over the pyre and extinguished its flames. To those present the event seemed miraculous; they took Habrocomes and brought him tò the ruler of Egypt and recounted the circumstances and explained the intercession of the Nile. When he heard what had happened the governor marveled, and he gave orders that Habrocomes should be under guard, indeed, in prison, but that every care should be shown him, ". . . until," he said, "we learn who this man is, and why it is that the gods are so concerned for him."

And so Habrocomes was kept in prison. But Psammis, who had purchased Anthia, resolved to depart to his own home, and made all things ready for the journey. His travels would take him to Upper Egypt and toward Ethiopia, where Hippothoos' robber band was located. Everything was in the best of order: there were many camels and asses and sumpter horses, there was an abundance of gold and also of silver, there were many garments, and Anthia too was carried along. She, when she had passed Alexandria and was now in Memphis, took position before the temple of Isis and prayed to her as follows: "O thou greatest of divinities, until now I have remained chaste, for I was believed to be thine, and I have preserved my marriage to

Habrocomes unsullied. But now I am on my way to India, a far stretch of land from Ephesus, far from the remains of Habrocomes. Either, then, deliver me, the unfortunate, from this place and return me to Habrocomes in life, or, if it is inexorably fated that we die apart from one another, accomplish this; let me remain chaste to him that is dead." Thus she prayed, and they proceeded on their way. They had passed through Coptos and were ascending the hills of Ethiopia, when Hippothoos fell upon them. Psammis himself he killed, and many of those with him; and he took possession of the chattels and made Anthia prisoner. When he had gathered together all the booty that had been taken, he carried it to the cave which they had designated as the depository of their acquisitions. Thither went Anthia also; she did not recognize Hippothoos, nor did Hippothoos recognize Anthia. And when he inquired of her who she might be and whence, she did not speak the truth, but declared that she was a native Egyptian and that her name was Memphitis. And so Anthia abode in the robbers' den with Hippothoos.

In the meanwhile the ruler of Egypt summoned Habrocomes and made detailed inquiries of him and learned his story. He pitied his lot and gave him money and promised to bring him to Ephesus. Habrocomes thanked the governor warmly for his deliverance, and requested that he be permitted instead to continue his search for Anthia. And so he received rich gifts and embarked upon a vessel and sailed for Italy, with a view to making inquiries concerning Anthia in that region. The ruler of Egypt, having now learned how Araxos had met his death, had Bitch brought to him and crucified her.

While Anthia was in the den, one of the robbers who kept watch over her, Anchialos by name, fell in love with her. This Anchialos was one of those who had followed Hippothoos from Syria, being a Laodicean by birth; Hippothoos had high regard for him, for he was energetic and had great authority in the robber band. When Anchialos fell in love with Anthia he first addressed her with persuasive words, thinking to himself that he would so win her and ask Hippothoos for her as a gift. But she rejected every argument and allowed nothing to trouble her, neither the cave nor bonds nor a menacing brigand. She still kept herself pure for Habrocomes, even though she believed him dead, and frequently would she cry out, whenever she was able to escape notice, "Habrocomes' wife only do I wish to remain, even if I must die, even if I must suffer affliction worse than I have suffered." Her attitude reduced Anchialos to greater distress, and the daily sight of Anthia added fuel to his love. And when he could no longer endure it he resolved to use violence. Once upon a night when Hippothoos with the others was gone on a foray, he arose against Anthia and attempted to force her. Finding herself in an ineluctable extremity, she seized a sword that was lying by and struck Anchialos, and the blow proved fatal. For while he was about to embrace her and kiss her and was leaning his whole body over her, she brought the point of the sword against his chest and so smote him. And so Anchialos received condign punishment for his wicked passion.

But Anthia was overwhelmed by fear for what she had done, and turned many plans over in her mind: now that she would kill herself—but she still had a vestige of hope for Habrocomes; now that she would flee from the cave—but this was impractical, for there was no easy road or anyone to give her guidance. And so she resolved to remain in the cave and endure whatever her fate would decree. So, then, did she pass that night, getting no sleep, her mind occupied with many thoughts. But when day came, there arrived Hippothoos and his company, and they saw Anchialos done to death and Anthia near the body. They conjectured what had happened, and when they questioned Anthia they learned all. Filled with wrath at the deed, they determined to avenge their deceased friend and considered various modes of punishing Anthia. One urged that she be killed and buried with the body of Anchialos, another that she be crucified. Hippothoos, who was sorely grieved at his comrade's death, devised a punishment yet more cruel. He bade them dig a trench, wide and deep, and in it cast Anthia together with two mastiffs, that she might thus meet with retribution appropriate to the brazenness of her crime. His men did as they were ordered, and Anthia was taken to the trench, and with her the dogs; these were of Egyptian breed, large and vicious and of terrible aspect. Now when they had cast them all into the pit, they placed wooden beams over it and heaped earth over them —the place was but little distant from the Nile—and set one of the robbers, Amphinomos by name, to stand guard over it.

This Amphinomos had even before this been smitten by Anthia, and now he had greater compassion for her and pitied her unhappy lot; and so he bethought him how she might prolong her life and how the dogs might be prevented from harming her. Each day, then, he removed the beams that closed the pit, and threw into it loaves of bread and provided water, and therewith exhorted Anthia to be of good cheer. The dogs, being well fed, did her no hurt, but became gentle and docile. But Anthia, taking thought of herself and reflecting upon her plight, lamented: "Woe is me for my afflictions! What punishment is this that I endure—a pit, a prison, mastiffs shut in with me—who are yet gentler far than the brigands. Now are my sufferings, Habrocomes, like yours. You too endured similar affliction; you were imprisoned in Tyre when I left you. Yet if you are alive these woes are nothing: someday, perhaps, we shall yet possess one another. But if you are dead, then it is in vain that I endeavor to live, in vain does my benefactor, whoever he may be, take pity on my lot." Thus she said, and she lamented incessantly. And so Anthia was immured in the pit with the dogs, and Amphinomos consoled her daily, and by feeding the dogs made them tractable.

5 *Now Habrocomes, pursuing his voyage from Egypt,* did not indeed reach Italy itself, for his ship was buffeted by a gale and strayed from its course, but was carried to Sicily and reached the large and handsome city of Syracuse. Arrived there, Habrocomes resolved to traverse the island and to make inquiries for Anthia; with luck he might obtain information. He took lodging near the sea in the house of an old man named Aigialeus, who was a fisherman by trade. Now this Aigialeus was a poor man and an alien, and scarcely able to keep himself by his trade; nevertheless he welcomed Habrocomes gladly, and

regarded him as his own son, and showed him singular affection. Once on a time, as result of their great familiarity with one another, Habrocomes recounted the whole story of his life to the old man, speaking of Anthia and his love and his wanderings; and then Aigialeus in turn began the narrative of his own life.

"Habrocomes, my child," said he, "I am neither Sicilian nor a native, but a Spartiate of Lacedaemonia, and among the most powerful and the wealthiest of the Spartans. When I was young I fell in love with a girl who was also Spartan, Thelxinoe by name, and Thelxinoe returned my love. When a festival vigil was being celebrated in the city, we came together one with the other, some deity guiding each of us on his way, and we took our joy of the object for which we had come together. For a space of time we consorted with one another, keeping our union secret, and we repeatedly swore to remain faithful to one another unto death. But some god must have begrudged us. While I was still in the cadet classification, her parents gave Thelxinoe in marriage to a young Spartan named Androcles, who was already, in fact, in love with Thelxinoe. At first the girl contrived numerous pretexts to postpone the marriage, and finally, when she found an opportunity to meet with me, she agreed to leave Lacedaemonia with me by night. We attired ourselves in the garb of young men, and I even shore Thelxinoe of her hair. On the very night of the marriage we departed from the city and proceeded to Argos and Corinth, and there we took ship and sailed to Sicily. When the Lacedaemonians learned of the flight they condemned us to death.

"We, for our part, lived our lives here, in actual want of necessities, yet in great happiness and as if we enjoyed abundance of all things, because we were together. Here, not long ago, Thelxinoe died. Her body is not buried; I keep it with me, and always I kiss it and consort with it." So saying, he led Habrocomes into an inner room and showed him Thelxinoe, who was quite an old woman; but in Aigialeus' eyes she was still the beautiful girl. Her body the old man had embalmed in the Egyptian manner, for he understood the technique. "With her, Habrocomes, my child," the old man continued, "I always talk as if she were alive, and I lie by her side, and I take my meals with her; and whenever I come home weary from my fishing she looks at me affectionately and comforts me. Not as she looks to you now does she appear in my sight. I conceive of her, my child, just as she was in Lacedaemonia, just as she was when we eloped; I conceive of her as she was on that festival vigil; I conceive of her as she was when we pledged our troth."

Even while Aigialeus was yet speaking Habrocomes began lamenting and said, "Ah, Anthia, girl unhappiest of all! When shall I ever find you, even a corpse? Aigialeus possesses a great solace for his life in the body of Thelxinoe, and now have I truly learned that true love has no limits of age. I am a vagabond over every land and sea, and yet have I not been able to hear any tidings of you. Oh, unhappy oracles! O Apollo, thou that hast foretold for us prophecies most grievous of all, do thou now take pity upon us and reveal the consummation of thine oracles!" So sorrowing, Habrocomes passed his time in Syracuse, and Aigialeus offered him comfort, and now he shared in Aigialeus' craft.

Now Hippothoos and his company had greatly enlarged their robber band, and they resolved to abandon Ethiopia and now to undertake larger enterprises. No longer did Hippothoos deem it sufficient to waylay individual travelers; now he would attack whole villages and cities. And so he mustered his company and loaded all his baggage (he possessed many pack animals and not a few camels), and left Ethiopia behind him. He proceeded toward Egypt and Alexandria, with the intention of continuing to Phoenicia and again to Syria. Anthia he now believed dead. But Amphinomos, who had kept guard over her in the pit, was deeply in love with her, and he could not abide being separated from the girl, both because of his affection for her and because of her imminent danger. He therefore did not follow Hippothoos, escaping notice because of the great multitude who did, and hid in a certain cave where he had cached a supply of provisions. When night fell Hippothoos and his company arrived at a village of Egypt called Areia, which they meant to ravage; but Amphinomos dug open the trench and brought Anthia out and spoke comforting words to her. When she was still frightened and still suspicious, he swore by the sun and by the gods of Egypt that he would preserve her chastity until such time as she herself should be persuaded and willingly consent. Anthia trusted Amphinomos' pledges and followed him; nor did the dogs leave them, for they had become used to their company and lovingly attended them. They came then to Coptos, and there they resolved to remain until Hippothoos and his company should be farther on their way. They took care also that the dogs should have plentiful food.

Hippothoos' band had now attacked the village of Areia, and had killed many of its inhabitants and burned their houses down. Their journey they continued not by the same land route but on the Nile. They had collected all the water craft from the intervening villages, and on these they embarked and sailed to Schedia, where they disembarked, and then passed through the remainder of Egypt along the banks of the Nile. In the meanwhile the ruler of Egypt had been informed concerning the raid on Areia and the activities of Hippothoos' brigands, and he learned also that they were proceeding to Ethiopia. He therefore mustered a large force of soldiers and appointed as their commander one of his own kinsmen, Polyidos by name, a young man charming in appearance and vigorous in action; him he sent against the brigands. This Polyidos and his force encountered Hippothoos' troop near Pelusium, and a battle between them took place immediately on the banks of the river. Many fell on either side, but when night came on the brigands turned in flight and were all butchered, some few prisoners being taken alive. Only Hippothoos, having thrown his arms away, escaped during the night and reached Alexandria. There he succeeded in escaping recognition, embarked on a vessel on the point of sailing, and put to sea. His great desire was to get to Sicily, for there he thought he could best avoid detection and most easily obtain a livelihood; he had heard that the island was both extensive and prosperous.

Polyidos did not think it sufficient merely to have vanquished the brigands he met in battle, but determined that all Egypt must be thoroughly searched and purged, and in particular he wished to apprehend Hippothoos or any of his company that might be at large. He took a portion of his soldiery, therefore, and those of the robbers that had been made prisoner, so that they might give information if any brigand were encountered, and sailed up the Nile, with the intention of proceeding as far as Ethiopia. The cities he passed he ransacked thoroughly, and in due course came also to Coptos, where Anthia was sojourning with Amphinomos. Anthia happened to be at home, but Amphinomos was recognized by the captive brigands, who informed Polyidos of his identity. Amphinomos was seized, and upon being interrogated recounted the story of Anthia. Upon hearing his account Polyidos ordered that Anthia be brought, and when she came he inquired who she was and whence. She on her part kept the truth concealed, but declared that she was an Egyptian and had been kidnaped by the brigands. As the conversation proceeded Polyidos too (who had a wife in Alexandria) fell deeply in love with Anthia. Being in love, he tried at first to persuade her with lavish promises; but at length, as they were approaching Alexandria and had got as far as Memphis, Polyidos attempted to use force upon Anthia. She contrived to escape and went to the temple of Isis, and there assumed the posture of a suppliant. "Do thou again save me, O my lady of Egypt," said she, "whom thou hast so frequently succored in time past. Let Polyidos, too, spare me, who for thy sake am keeping myself chaste for Habrocomes." Now Polyidos revered the goddess and also loved Anthia, whose lot moved his compassion; he therefore approached the temple unattended and swore that he would never violate Anthia and never commit any outrage against her, but would preserve her chaste for as long as she herself should wish. Sufficient for his love would it be if he could merely look at her and speak with her. By these pledges was Anthia persuaded, and she quitted the temple.

Since it had been decided to take repose in Memphis for three days, Anthia visited the shrine of Apis. This is the most celebrated temple in Egypt, and here those who wish receive oracles from the god. When the visitor has offered his prayers and made his petition to the god, he himself leaves the sanctuary, and in front of the temple Egyptian children, speaking some things in prose and some in verse, declare details of future events. Anthia, too, made her obeisance to Apis, and said, "O thou most benevo-lent of deities to man, thou who dost show compassion to strang-ers, take thou pity too upon my wretched lot, and declare unto me a true oracle concerning Habrocomes. For if I am yet des-tined to see him and receive him as my husband, I shall pa-tiently continue to live, but if he has died it were well for me, too, to be quit of this troublesome life." So she said, and, suf-fused with tears, she issued from the temple. As she did so the children playing before the temple called out altogether, "An-thia shall soon recover her own husband Habrocomes." When she heard this she became more cheerful and rendered thanks to the gods. And then, in Polyidos' company, she proceeded to Alexandria.

But his wife had learned that Polyidos was bringing back a girl with whom he was in love, and she was afraid that she would be surpassed in rivalry with the newcomer. To Polyidos she said nothing, but in her own heart she deliberated how she might avenge herself upon the woman she thought was sub-verting her marriage. Now Polyidos had gone to the ruler of Egypt to render an account of his campaign, and then was occu-pied at his headquarters, administering the duties of his office. In his absence Rhenaia (for so was Polyidos' wife called) sum-moned Anthia, who was left at home, and tore her clothing and disfigured her person. "Wicked woman," said she, "you plotter against my marriage, it is in vain that you seemed fair to Polyi-dos; that beauty will profit you little. You may have been able to allure robbers and to lie with many young bravos when they were all well drunk. But the bed of Rhenaia you will never in-sult with impunity." So saying, she shore Anthia's hair off and threw her into chains and delivered her to a certain faithful slave named Clytos, with orders to embark her upon a ship, carry her to Italy, and there sell her to a brothel keeper. "Now," she cried, "you will be able to fill your lust to satiety." And so Anthia was led off by Clytos, weeping and wailing, and she said, "Ah, perfidious beauty, ah, ill-starred charm, why do you abide with me to afflict me, why have you caused me so many woes? Were not burials and murders and chains and brigands enough? Must I now be displayed before a brothel, and at a whoremaster's bidding dispose of that chastity which up to now I have preserved for Habrocomes? But oh, my master," said she falling at Clytos' knees, "do not, I pray you, carry me away to foul punishment, but kill me yourself. I cannot tolerate a whoremonger as master. My way of life, believe me, is chaste." So she besought him, and Clytos took pity upon her. So Anthia was carried off to Italy. When Polyidos came home Rhenaia told him that Anthia had run away; and Anthia's past conduct induced him to believe her.

But Anthia was put ashore at Tarentum, a city in Italy, where Clytos, faithful to Rhenaia's bidding, sold her to a brothel keeper. When he perceived such beauty as he had never before seen, he thought the girl would bring him great profit. Some days of repose he gave her to refresh herself from the voyage and from the ill-treatment she had suffered at the hands of Rhenaia. Clytos returned to Alexandria and reported to Rhenaia that her orders had been carried out.

Now Hippothoos, too, had completed his voyage and landed in Sicily—not at Syracuse, however, but at Taormina—and there he looked out for some opportunity to procure the necessities of life. As for Habrocomes, as his stay in Syracuse was prolonged, he fell into a state of discouragement and helplessness because he could find neither news of Anthia nor any means of returning safe to his own country. He therefore resolved to leave Sicily and sail over to Italy, and from there, if he failed to find the object of his search, to make the sad voyage back to Ephesus. By now the parents of both and indeed all the Ephesians sorrowed deeply, for neither had any messenger nor any letters from the young couple reached them, though they sent agents in all directions to make inquires after them. Despair and old age rendering the parents incapable of further endurance, they found their release from life. Habrocomes was now on his way to Italy. As for Leucon and Rhode, the comrades of Habrocomes and Anthia, their master had died in Xanthos and had bequeathed to them his very considerable property. They resolved to sail to Ephesus, imagining that their masters had already returned thither in safety, and being themselves satiated with the tribulations of sojourning abroad.

And so they put all their possessions aboard ship and sailed for Ephesus. After a few days' voyage they put in at Rhodes, and there they learned that Habrocomes and Anthia were not yet safely returned home, and that their parents had died. They resolved then not to continue to Ephesus but for the present to sojourn in Rhodes, until they should obtain some tidings of their young masters.

Now the brothel master who had purchased Anthia compelled her, after some days had passed, to display herself before his establishment. And so, bedizening her in ornate garments and with much gilt, he exposed her to public view at the door of the stew. She then cried out bitterly, "Alas for my afflictions! Are not my previous misfortunes sufficient—prison, brigands? Must I even be forced to play the whore? Ah, beauty deservedly contemned, why do you cling to me so unseasonably? But why do I utter these lamentations? Why do I not rather find some device by which I may preserve that chastity which I have guarded up to the present?" Amid these plaints she was brought to the brothel, her master now offering encouragement and now uttering threats. When she arrived at the stew and was put on display there was a great concourse of men who marveled at her beauty, and many were eager to pay the fee and satisfy their lust.

Finding herself in this ineluctable extremity, Anthia invented a means of escape. She fell to the ground, relaxing her limbs, and imitated the state of those who suffer from what men call "the sacred disease." All present were touched by pity and fear. They forbore their desire for intercourse, but rather wished to minister to Anthia. The brothel keeper realized that his plans had miscarried; believing that the girl was truly ill, he took her to his house and made her lie down, and tended her. When she seemed to come back to herself he asked her the cause of her illness. And Anthia said, "Even before this, master, I wished to tell you my trouble and to explain what had happened, but I kept it secret because I was ashamed. But now it is no longer difficult for me to speak to you, for you have already learned all about me. Once, when I was still a child, I strayed away from my family during the celebration of a festival vigil, and came upon the grave of a man who had recently died. There it seemed to me that someone leapt out of the grave and tried to lay hold of me. I shrieked and tried to flee. The man was frightful to look upon, and his voice was more horrible still. Finally, when day broke, he let me go, but he struck me on the chest and said that he had cast this disease into me. Beginning with that day I have been afflicted with that calamity, which takes divers forms and divers occasions. But I beg of you, master, do not be angry with me; I am not to blame for this situation. You will be able to sell me, and lose no penny of the price you paid for me." When the brothel keeper heard this he was greatly annoyed, but he forgave the girl, believing that her epilepsy was not of her own choosing.

And so Anthia, simulating illness, was nursed at the house of the brothel keeper. Now Habrocomes had sailed from Sicily and made land at Nuceria in Italy, but he was at a loss for some occupation to supply his needs. At first he went about searching for Anthia, for it was she that was the object of all his life and all his vagabondage; but when he could find nothing (for the girl was in the house of the brothel keeper in Tarentum) he hired himself out to some stonecutters. To him this work was very laborious, for his body was not inured to undergo toil so intense and demanding. Thus he found himself in a miserable state, and often did he bewail his own lot, saying, "Look now, Anthia, at your Habrocomes, a laborer in a toilsome trade, his body reduced to slavery. If I could have any hope of finding you and of living the rest of my life with you, that would comfort me with the best of all solace. But now, unhappy that I am, perhaps I toil for vanity and folly, perhaps somewhere you lie dead, out of yearning for your Habrocomes. But of this, my dearest, I am certain: never at all, even in death, have you forgotten me." Thus he grieved, and with pain bore his toil.

But to Anthia, as she lay sleeping in Tarentum, a dream appeared. It seemed to her that she was with Habrocomes, she in all her beauty and he in all his beauty, and that it was the season of the beginning of their love. There appeared then another woman, also beautiful, who dragged Habrocomes away from her. Then, when Habrocomes cried out and called her by name Anthia awoke and the dream came to an end. When she reflected on the vision she leapt up and lamented sore, and believed that what she had seen was true. "Woe is me for my afflictions!" she cried. "Here am I enduring every manner of hardship, and experiencing every variety of calamity in my misery, and inventing expedients beyond a woman's powers to preserve my chastity for Habrocomes; but you have now found some other woman fair—that, surely, is what my dream signifies. Why, then, do I linger in life? Why do I afflict myself? Better it were to perish, and to be quit of this vile existence, to be quit, too, of this unseemly disgrace and perilous servitude. But if Habrocomes has in truth transgressed his oaths, may the gods refrain from punishing him: perhaps it was under duress that he did what he did. But for me it is seemly to die chaste." Thus she said in her anguish, and she sought some expedient to compass her death.

At Taormina things went hard at first with Hippothoos the Perinthian, for he found it difficult to get a livelihood; but in course of time an old woman fell in love with him, and, being constrained by poverty, he married the old woman. With her he lived for a short space, and then she died and he succeeded to her great fortune and opulent possessions. He now had a large train of slaves, a sumptuous supply of clothing, and a lavish collection of household goods. He then resolved to voyage to Italy in order to purchase handsome slaves and maidservants and other articles of luxury, as was becoming to a nabob. The memory of Habrocomes also was ever present to him, and he prayed that he might find him, for he made it his ambition to share his life and his possessions with him. And so he set sail and arrived in Italy. There attended him a young man of high Sicilian birth, Clisthenes by name, who shared in all Hippothoos' affluence, for he was a very handsome young man.

Now that brothel keeper, when it seemed that Anthia had recovered her health, bethought him how he might sell her, and so he took her to the market place and exhibited her to purchasers. Meanwhile Hippothoos was walking about the city of Tarentum, seeking some beautiful object that he might acquire. He caught sight of Anthia and recognized her; the event astonished him greatly, and he turned the matter over in his mind:

"Is she not the girl for whom I once dug a pit in Egypt, and immured therein with mastiffs, to avenge the murder of my friend Anchialos? What does this transformation mean? How did she save her life? How could she have escaped from that pit? What is this miraculous deliverance?" So saying, he approached, as if desirous of making a purchase, and when he stood near her he said, "Tell me, girl, do you not know Egypt? Did you not fall into the hands of robbers there? Did you not undergo other afflictions in that country? Do not be afraid to speak; I recognize you."

When Anthia heard mention of Egypt, and called to mind Anchialos and the robber band and the pit, she groaned and lamented, and then she looked steadfastly upon Hippothoos, whom she was altogether unable to recognize, and said, "I have indeed suffered many terrible afflictions in Egypt, stranger, whoever you may be, and I did fall into the hands of robbers. But how," she continued, "do you come to know my story? Whence do you say that you know me, that am so hapless? Much noised, indeed, and known to fame are the sufferings I have undergone; but you I do not know at all." What Hippothoos heard confirmed his recognition the more surely; for the moment he held his peace, and bought her of the brothel keeper and took her to his own quarters. There he bade her take heart and declared who he was and recalled the events in Egypt; he also explained the source of his wealth, and how he had made his own escape. She then begged his forgiveness, exculpating herself for the slaying of Anchialos by his unchaste attempt upon her, and she explained about the pit and Amphinomos and the docility of the dogs and her deliverance. Hippothoos took pity upon her, but never inquired who she was. As a result of their daily association Hippothoos, too, conceived a desire for Anthia and wished to have congress with her, and made her many promises. She on her part at first refused him upon the allegation that she was unworthy of so lordly a bed. But finally, when Hippothoos was urgent and she knew not what to do, she deemed it nobler to declare what she had as yet never revealed to him than to violate her pledges to Habrocomes. Therefore did she speak of Habrocomes, of Ephesus, of their love, of their calamities, of their captivities; and incessantly she moaned for Habrocomes. But when Hippothoos heard that she was indeed Anthia and the wife of the man dearest to him in all the world, he saluted her and bade her take heart, and he explained his own friendship for Habrocomes. Her he kept chaste at home, showing her every consideration out of respect to Habrocomes; he himself prosecuted a diligent investigation to find the whereabouts of Habrocomes.

Habrocomes at first worked at his painful labor in Nuceria, but at length, when he could no longer endure the toil, he resolved to take ship and sail for Ephesus. One night, then, he went down to the sea and embarked on the first boat ready to sail. This was bound back to Sicily, whence Habrocomes thought he would proceed to Crete, Cyprus, and Rhodes, and thence make his way to Ephesus; upon so long a voyage he hoped he might learn some news of Anthia. And so he sailed, with very scant supply of provisions, and arrived at Sicily, the first stage of his journey. There he found that his sometime host, Aigialeus, had died; he offered libations at his tomb and wept for him as was due, and then took ship again. He skirted Crete and arrived at Cyprus, where he lingered a few days and offered prayer to the ancestral goddess of the Cypriots. Then he sailed again and reached Rhodes, where he took lodging near the harbor. When he now found himself near Ephesus the memory of all his afflictions recurred to his mind. He thought of his country, his parents, Anthia, his servants, and he groaned deeply and said, "Alas for my tribulations! To Ephesus I come solitary, and I must show myself to my parents without Anthia. Vain, woe is me, is the voyage upon which I sail, and the story I have to recount may meet with little credence, for I have no witness to my trials. But endure manfully, Habrocomes, and when you are come to Ephesus continue in life until such time as you can raise a tomb for Anthia and bewail her and offer her libations, and then go and join her." Thus he said, and he wandered about the city distracted, at a loss for news of Anthia, at a loss for sustenance.

Now Leucon and Rhode, who were passing their time in Rhodes, dedicated a votive offering in the temple of the sun, near the golden panoply which Anthia and Habrocomes had dedicated. They set up a pillar with an inscription in honor of Habrocomes and Anthia in letters of gold, and they inscribed upon it also the names of the donors, Leucon and Rhode. Upon this pillar Habrocomes chanced, when he came to the temple to offer prayer to the god. He read the inscription and recognized the donors, and when he perceived the loyal good will of his servants and saw the panoply near by, he sat him down by the pillar and lamented: "How everything conspires to my misfortune!" he moaned. "Here I have come to the limit of my life and to the recollection of all my calamities. Lo, this panoply I dedicated with Anthia, and with Anthia I sailed from Ephesus, whither I now return without her. This pillar our companions dedicated for the happiness of us both: why then am I now alone? Where shall I find all that is dearest to me?" So he said in his lamentation.

In the meanwhile Leucon and Rhode had come to offer their customary prayers to the god, and they perceived Habrocomes sitting beside the pillar and gazing at the panoply; they did not recognize him, and wondered why a stranger should linger near the offerings of others. Then did Leucon address him: "Young man, what is the meaning of your sitting by votive offerings which do not belong to you and groaning and lamenting? What is your concern with these dedications? What connection have you with those whose names are inscribed upon them?" Habrocomes replied and said, " 'Tis for me, for me that Leucon and Rhode have made this offering. It is they whom, next to Anthia, I, the unfortunate Habrocomes, prayerfully yearn to see." When Leucon and Rhode heard these words they were struck dumb, but by degrees they recovered, and from his posture and voice, from what he said and his mention of Anthia, they recognized him and fell at his feet. Then they recounted all that had befallen them—their journey from Tyre to Syria, the fury of Manto, their transfer and sale in Lycia, the death of their owner, their acquisition of property, and their arrival in Rhodes. Thence they took Habrocomes to the house where they themselves sojourned, and delivered over to him all that they had acquired, and they took care of him and tended him, and they encouraged him to take heart. But to him nothing had value in comparison with Anthia, and for her he grieved at every turn. And so Habrocomes passed his time in Rhodes with his companions, deliberating what he should do.

But Hippothoos resolved to carry Anthia from Italy to Ephesus, in order to deliver her to her parents and there make inquiry concerning Habrocomes. All his possessions, therefore, he embarked upon a large Ephesian vessel and put to sea with Anthia. Their voyage was very prosperous, and in a few days they put in at Rhodes, landing when it was still night. There Hippothoos took lodging with a certain old woman, Althaea by name, near the sea, and put Anthia in the care of his hostess. That night he gave to repose, and the following day they busied themselves with preparations to sail on.

But the Rhodians were celebrating a magnificent public festival in honor of the sun; there was a procession and a sacrifice and a great host of citizens making festival. Leucon and Rhode were also there in attendance, not so much to participate in the festival as to make inquires to learn tidings of Anthia. Then came to the shrine Hippothoos, bringing Anthia with him. And when she looked upon the votive offerings and fell into a reverie of the past, she said, "O thou Sun who dost look beneficently upon all mankind, passing only me, the unfortunate, when I was in Rhodes aforetime happily did I do obeisance to thee, and I offered sacrifices with Habrocomes, and even thought me blessed. Now I am a slave instead of free, a miserable captive instead of a happy girl, and I go to Ephesus alone, and must show myself to my kinsmen with no Habrocomes." Thus she said, and she wept copious tears, and she begged Hippothoos to permit her to shear some of her own tresses and consecrate them to the sun and utter a prayer for Habrocomes. Hippothoos consented, and so she cut off as many of her locks as she could, and when she found a fitting moment, when all visitors had departed, she dedicated her offering, inscribing upon it: "ON BEHALF OF HER HUSBAND, HABROCOMES, ANTHIA DEDICATES HER HAIR TO THE GOD." When she had done this and had offered her prayer, she departed with Hippothoos.

For a while Leucon and Rhode had attended the procession,

but now they entered the temple and saw the dedication and recognized their mistress' name. First they caressed the hair and sorrowed as if they were looking upon Anthia herself. Then they hurried about, if perchance they might avail to find herself (for the Rhodian folk knew their names from their former sojourn). That day they found nothing, and so they returned home and reported to Habrocomes what they saw in the temple. The strangeness of the occurrence agitated Habrocomes to the soul, but he was now hopeful that he would find Anthia. On the morrow the weather was not fair for sailing and Anthia again came to the temple with Hippothoos, and sat down by the votive offerings, and wept and sighed. While she was so engaged Leucon and Rhode entered the temple; Habrocomes they had left at home because he was downhearted on the same account. When they entered they saw Anthia, whom as yet they did not recognize; but the love she displayed, her tears, the offerings, the inscribed names, her figure, all assisted their conjecture, and so gradually they came to recognize her. Thereupon they fell at her knees and lay there speechless; she for her part wondered who they were and what they wished, for she had never hoped she would see Leucon and Rhode. But when they came to themselves they cried, "Mistress! Anthia! We are your slaves, Leucon and Rhode, who shared your travel abroad and your capture by the robbers. But what chance has brought you here? Take heart, mistress, Habrocomes is safe, and he is here, and he laments for you constantly." Anthia was so struck by what she heard that she lost her power of speech. With difficulty did she collect herself; she embraced them and saluted them and desired to hear every detail that concerned Habrocomes.

When it became known that Anthia and Habrocomes were found all the Rhodians flocked together in a crowd. Hippothoos, too, was now present; he was known to Leucon and Rhode, and himself learned who they were. Now was everything consummated to their satisfaction—except that Habrocomes himself was not yet aware of it! They ran just as they were to the house. But Habrocomes, when he heard from some Rhodian that Anthia was found, ran through the midst of the city shouting, "Anthia!"—like a man bereft of his wits did he run. And he did meet Anthia and those with her near the temple of Isis, and a great concourse of Rhodians followed after them. When they saw one another they recognized each other immediately, for this was their very soul's desire. They embraced one another, and sank to the ground. Many and various emotions commingled held them fast—pleasure, pain, fear, memory of the past, apprehension for the future. But the populace of Rhodes shouted their felicitations and uttered cries of joy and invoked the great goddess, Isis, saying, "Again we behold Habrocomes and Anthia, the beautiful pair." And they, when they recovered from their agitation, rose up and entered the shrine of Isis, saying, "O thou greatest Goddess, we thank thee for our deliverance. Because of thee, who art to us most precious of all, we have recovered one another and ourselves." In ecstasy they moved through the sacred precinct and humbled themselves before the altar.

Then did Leucon and his friends conduct them to his house, and Hippothoos transferred all his belongings to the same house, and they were ready to set sail for Ephesus. And when they had offered sacrifice during that day and had well feasted, many and varied were the tales each had to tell, so much had each suffered, so much had each done, and they protracted the banquet on and on, for it was after a weary time that they were now reunited. And when night was fallen they all went to their rest as fortune decreed—Leucon with Rhode; Hippothoos and the young man from Sicily who had followed him when he went to Italy, the handsome Clisthenes; and Anthia went to rest with Habrocomes.

Now when the others were all asleep and profound quiet reigned, Anthia embraced Habrocomes, and wept, saying, "My husband and my lord, I have recovered you after my long wandering over land and sea. I have escaped the threats of brigands, the plots of pirates, the outrages of brothel keepers, and chains, and pits, and beams, and poisons, and burial. But I come to you now, Habrocomes, my soul's master, just as I was when I departed from Tyre for Syria. No one has persuaded me to sin against you, neither Moeris in Syria, nor Perilaos in Cilicia, nor, in Egypt, Psammis and Polyidos, nor Anchialos in Ethiopia, nor my owner in Tarentum; nay, I have employed every device to preserve chastity and have remained pure for you. But you now, Habrocomes, have you abided chaste, or has some rival fair taken precedence over me? Or has anyone forced you to be forgetful of your pledges and of me?" Thus she said, and she kissed him close. But Habrocomes replied, "I swear to you by this day we have so ardently desired and so barely attained, that neither has any maiden appeared fair in my sight, nor has any other woman that I have seen won my favor; you receive Habrocomes back just such as you left him in the prison in Tyre."

With such protestations to one another they passed all that night, and easily did they persuade one another, for such was their desire. When day broke they embarked upon their ship, upon which they had laden their posesssions, and all the multitude of the Rhodians came to escort them and wish them good speed. Hippothoos, too, departed with them, taking his goods and Clisthenes. And in a few days they completed their voyage and landed at Ephesus. All the city had learned of their deliverance in advance; and when they disembarked, immediately and just as they were they proceeded to the temple of Artemis and offered many prayers and performed various sacrifices, but in particular they dedicated to the goddess an inscription which recounted all that they had suffered and all that they had done. And when they had accomplished this they ascended to the city and raised large tombs for their parents (who, as it happened, had died by reason of old age and despair), and the remainder of their lives they passed with one another, keeping, as it were, continuous festival. And Leucon and Rhode shared all the good things that their comrades had; and Hippothoos, too, resolved to pass the remainder of his days in Ephesus. For Hyperanthes he had raised a great tomb when he was in Lesbos, and now Hippothoos adopted Clisthenes as his son and lived in Ephesus with Habrocomes and Anthia.

Of Xenophon's Ephesian Tale of
Anthia and Habrocomes
the end.

The Hunters
of Euboea
BY DIO CHRYSOSTOM

The story I shall tell is not a thing I heard from others, but what I myself saw. Wordiness is an old man's way: it is not easy to put a graybeard off once he has begun to talk. But maybe it is a vagabond's way too. The reason is old men and vagabonds alike have lived through much and like to recall their experiences. What I shall tell about are some men I met practically in the heart of Greece, and the kind of life they lived.

I happened to be sailing across from Chios with some fishermen. Summer voyaging was over and our craft was tiny, so when a storm blew up we barely got safe to the Hollows of Euboea. The fishermen ran their boat up on a rough shingle under the cliffs and smashed it, then went off to join some purple fishers who were moored at a nearby spur. Their thought was to stay there and work with the purple fishers. I was left all alone. I knew no city where I might find shelter, and so roamed down by the sea in the hope of spying some boat sailing by or riding at anchor. For a considerable piece I rambled on without seeing a living creature, but then did I spy a deer which had tumbled down the cliff and was gasping its life away on the shingle, where the waves were sweeping over it. After a bit I thought I heard dogs barking above me, but it was hard to be sure on account of the noise from the sea. I went forward and with great exertion climbed the height, from which I saw the actual dogs, baffled and running in circles; it was they, I conjectured, who had forced the creature to jump down the cliff. Presently I saw a man. By his looks and dress I judged he was a hunter. He had a healthy beard to his face, not just the ordinary shabby shag behind that Homer says the Euboeans who went to Troy had. Homer was having his joke at the expense

129

of the Euboeans, I am sure: while the other Achaeans made a fine show the Euboeans were half tonsured.

The man accosted me: "Stranger, have you seen a startled deer hereabouts?" "Yonder he is now in the surf," said I to him, and then took him and pointed it out to him. He dragged it out of the surf and flayed its skin off with his knife, with me trying to help as best I could. Then he lopped off the hind-quarters to take home with the hide. He invited me to come along too, and share his venison feast. His house, he said, was no great distance off. "And then in the morning," he continued, "after a good sleep, you will go down to the sea. This is no sail-ing weather. But don't be uneasy. For my part I should be pleased enough if the wind stopped even after five days—but that is hardly likely when the Euboean mountains are so weighed down with clouds; you can see how the peaks are cov-ered." At that he asked where I had sailed from, how I had come to land at that spot, and whether my boat had not been wrecked. "It was a little boat," said I; "some fishermen were ferrying across in it, and I went with them on an errand of my own. But the boat was wrecked when it grounded." "What else could it have done?" said he. "You see how wild and rugged this island is on its sea side. These are what are called the Hol-lows of Euboea. No ship driven ashore here can survive, and very rarely are any passengers saved unless their boat is, as yours was, very light. But come along and do not be afraid. For the present you must refresh yourself after your harrowing trial. Tomorrow we shall take what measures we can for your safety. Now that I have come to know you, you look to me like a city man, not a sailor or farm hand. Yet you are thin and poorly; perhaps something else ails you."

I was glad enough to follow him. I could not think he meant me any harm, for all I had was a shabby coat. In similar situa-tions it has been my repeated experience (and I have traveled a good deal), and emphatically so in the present instance, that poverty is in fact a great and inviolable asylum. People are less likely to wrong a poor man than a herald with his badge of immunity. So I followed my guide without misgiving.

We had about five miles to go, and as we walked he told me

all about himself and the kind of life he led with his wife and children. "There are two of us, stranger," said he, "who live in the same place. Each is married to the sister of the other, and we have children, both boys and girls. We live by hunting for the most part, but we work a bit of land, too. The place is not really ours; we neither inherited nor bought it. Our fathers were free men, indeed, but just as poor as we. They were herdsmen, and kept cattle for a rich man who lived on this island. This man owned many herds of horses and cows, many sheep, many fine fields, many other valuables, and all these hills. When he died his property was confiscated—people say the emperor did him in for his property. His herds were immediately driven off to be butchered, and with them our own few head of cattle. Nobody paid our wages. For the time we could only stay where we had been keeping the cattle. We had built huts and a wooden corral for the calves. It was not very big or very sturdy, but a makeshift for the summer. In the winter we used to graze in the plain, where we had plenty of pasturage and a good store of fodder, but in the summer we would drive the cattle to the hills. It was this place our fathers chose for their steading. The land slopes down on either side, and there is a deep, shady valley. In the middle of it was a creek so smooth that cows and even calves could wade in it. The water was supplied by a nearby spring, and was plentiful and pure, and all summer a breeze blew through the valley. The surrounding glades were lush and though they were well watered they bred never a fly or anything else to trouble the cattle. There were straight, tall trees with lovely spacious meadows spreading under them. Throughout the summer everything was covered with luxuriant vegetation, and forage was not far to seek. That is why they regularly settled their herds there.

"There, then, our fathers stayed on in their huts, waiting to find some employer or work. They supported themselves by a tiny plot they cultivated near the byre; being well manured, it satisfied their needs. With no cows to keep them busy they turned to hunting; sometimes by themselves, sometimes with dogs. Two shepherd dogs had followed the cattle for quite a distance, but when they could not find their masters they left the herd and returned to the huts. At first these dogs would merely follow along, as if they had some different business. If they sighted wolves they would chase them a piece, but they were not interested in boars or deer. But if ever they sighted a bear, early or late, they would make a stand yelping and fending him off as if it were a man they were fighting. When they had got the taste of blood and had got used to pork and venison, they learned new tricks late in life and got a liking for meat instead of bread. If any game was taken they gorged; if not they starved, and so they paid more attention to hunting and chased everything they sighted. Somehow or other they managed to pick up scents and trails, and from shepherd dogs they turned into hunting hounds, late learners, to be sure, and a little slow.

"When winter came on there was no work in sight; they could find none in town or in any village. So they boarded up the walls of their huts and made their yard stouter and so got through the winter. Now they worked the whole of their plot, and winter made hunting easier. Tracks marked on damp ground are clearer, and the snow makes them visible at a distance. This made a kind of highway to the game, and there was no need to bother with searching it out. The animals, too, were sluggish, and waited to be caught; rabbits and deer could actually be taken in their lairs. From that time on our fathers continued that kind of life and wanted no other. And they got us married, each giving his daughter to the other's son. Both died about a year ago; the years of their lives were many, but their bodies were still rugged and youthful and vigorous. Of our mothers only mine is still living.

"My comrade has never been down to town at all, though he is fifty years old. I have been down twice, once as a boy with my father, when we still had the cows, and later when a man came to ask for money. He imagined we had some, and ordered us to come to the city with him. We hadn't any money, and swore we hadn't: we'd have given it to him if we had had any. We gave him the best hospitality we could, and made him a present of two deerskins. It was I that went to the city with him, for he said that one of us must by all means go and explain how things were.

"The sights were like those I had seen on my other trip. There were many large houses and a strong wall outside, and high, square rooms on the wall. There were many boats riding at anchor, completely motionless, as if it were a lake. There is nothing like that here where you landed, and that is why ships are wrecked. That is what I saw. It is a great crowd of people shut into the same place and a frightening roar and shouting; I thought they were all fighting with one another. Well, the man brought me before certain magistrates and said with a laugh, 'This is the fellow you sent me for. He has nothing but his long hair and a hut of very strong timbers.' The magistrates strode to the theater, and I with them. The theater is a sort of hollow valley, not, however, straight up and down, but half round. It is not a natural formation, but built of stones. You are probably laughing at me for explaining what you know perfectly well.

"At first the crowd spent a long time attending to other business. They kept shouting, sometimes amiably and with good temper, when they wished to applaud, but sometimes angrily and in bad temper. Their angry fits were awful. The people they shouted at were terrified; some of them ran around begging mercy and others flung their cloaks off for fear. Once I myself was almost knocked over by the shouting: it was as if a tidal wave or clap of thunder had broken over me. Some men would step forward and some rise in their places and address the crowd. Some said a few words, others made long speeches. To some the crowd would listen for quite a long while; with others they grew angry as soon as they opened their mouths, and would not let them so much as cheep.

"At last they settled down, and in an interval of quiet they brought me forward. One man spoke out: 'This man, gentlemen, is one of those who have been exploiting our public domain for many years, and not he alone, but his father before him. They graze our hills, they farm, they hunt, they build many houses, they set out vines, and they have many other good things, but they pay no one any rent for the land, nor have they received it from the state as a gift. For what services could they ever have received it? They hold in possession what is ours, and though they wax rich on it they never perform any public service whatever nor pay any share of their income in tax. Without paying taxes or contributing the required services they go blithely on as if they were exempted for benefactions to the city. I verily believe,' he continued, 'that they have never even come here before.' I shook my head, and the crowd laughed when they saw. The laughter infuriated the speaker, and he abused me for it. Then he turned back to the crowd and said, 'If you approve of these things so heartily, we had all better lose no time in looting the public property. Some can take the city's money, as certain persons are surely doing this moment, and some can squat upon the land without your consent, if you are going to let these beasts hold as dowry more than two hundred and fifty acres of fine land, from which you could collect three Attic quarts of grain for each citizen.'

"When I heard this I laughed as hard as I could. But the crowd did not laugh as before: now they raised a tumult. The man grew angry and gave me a terrible stare. 'Do you notice the sarcasm and impudence of that scum?' he said. 'Do you mark how brazenly he laughs? I am minded to jail him, and his partner too. The two, I understand, are ringleaders of the gang that has grabbed virtually all the land in our hills. Nor do these same fellows, I am sure, keep their hands from the wrecks that are from time to time cast up on rocks of Caphereus; they live just above the place. How else would they acquire such valuable fields—whole villages, I had better say—and such quantities of cattle, work animals, and slaves? Perhaps you have noticed how shabby his smock is and the skin he has put on to come here, on purpose to deceive you into thinking he is a pauper and has nothing. For my part,' said he, 'when I look at him I am almost frightened, as I imagine I should be if I saw Nauplius himself coming from Caphereus. I verily believe he lights beacons on the heights to lure mariners onto the rocks.' As he was saying these things and much more besides, the crowd growled savagely. I was at a loss, and feared they might do me some mischief.

"There came forward then another speaker, a kindly man, to judge from the words he spoke and from his appearance. First he asked the people to be quiet, and they did fall silent.

And then in a gentle voice he told them that people who worked idle land and put it into condition committed no wrong, but on the contrary might justly receive commendation. Not those who cultivated public land and planted it should be penalized, but those who ruined it. 'Even now, gentlemen,' he said, 'almost two thirds of our country is desolate because of neglect and depopulation. I, too, own many acres, as I imagine others here do, not only in the hills but also in the plains, and if anyone were willing to farm them I should not only let him do so gratis, but gladly pay him money besides. Obviously their value is increased, and besides land that is lived on and worked makes an agreeable sight. Wasteland is not only a useless encumbrance to its owner but a pitiful advertisement of the master's misfortune.

" 'In my judgment, therefore, you should rather encourage as many other citizens as you can to take some of the public land and work it. Those who have some capital should take more, and the poor as much as each can manage. Thus your land would be worked, and the citizens who volunteer relieved of two great evils, idleness and poverty. For ten years let them hold the land without charges, and after that period let them pay a small assessment on their tilth, but none on livestock. If a non-citizen works the land he too should pay nothing for five years, and thereafter twice the sum citizens pay. And any non-citizen who works as many as fifty acres ought to be given citizenship, in order to encourage the greatest possible number. As things are now the land outside our very gates has run wild and is extremely ugly, as if it were some deep wilderness and not the approach of a city. Inside the walls, furthermore, most of the land is sown or grazed. In view of this,' said he, 'the conduct of our orators is very strange. Against the hard-working people of Caphereus, in a remote corner of Euboea, they trump up charges, but they see no harm in men plowing up the gymnasium and grazing cattle in the market square. See for yourselves: your gymnasium they have made into a grainfield, and the stalks have completely hidden the Heracles and many other statues; heroes and gods are covered. Every day sheep belonging to the previous speaker take over the market square at dawn and graze around the senate house and administration buildings. When strangers first come to our city some of them laugh at it and others pity it.' When the crowd heard this they directed their fury against the first speaker and raised a clamor.

" 'That sort of thing the man does himself,' he continued, 'but he holds that ordinary folk who struggle for livelihood ought to be jailed. Obviously he intends that no one shall work in future; those outside the city must turn highwaymen and those inside footpads. I propose that we remit to these men what they themselves have created. For the future let them pay a moderate tax, but they must not be obligated for arrears. They have earned remission by putting under cultivation land that was deserted and useless. If they wish to put down a price for the land, we must sell it to them for less than to others.' After this speech the first man spoke in rebuttal, and there were harsh words on both sides. At length I too was bidden to say whatever I liked.

" 'What kind of thing must I say?' said I. 'Speak to what has been said,' said a man in the audience. 'Then I say,' said I, 'that there is no truth at all in what he said. When he babbled on about fields and villages and the like I thought, sirs, that I must be dreaming. We have no villages or horses or asses or cattle. I wish we did have all the fine things he mentions: we could give some to you and be rich ourselves. But what we do have is enough for us, and if you want any of it, take it. Take it all, if you like; we shall get another supply.' They applauded what I said, and the magistrate then asked me what we could give the people. 'Four very fine deerskins,' said I. Most of the people laughed, and the magistrate was vexed at me. 'I offer the deer because the bearskins are tough,' said I, 'and the goatskins are not their equal; some are old and some are small. But if you like take them too.' Again the man was vexed, and called me a stupid field hand. 'There you go talking about fields again,' said I. 'Didn't you hear me say that we have no fields?'

"The magistrate now asked whether we would be willing to contribute one hundred pounds each. 'We do not weigh our meat,' I said, 'but whatever it amounts to we will give it to you. A little of it is salted down, and the rest is smoked, but nearly as

good. There are sides of bacon and venison and other fine meat.'
There was an uproar indeed at this point, and they said I was
lying. But the man went on to ask me whether we had any grain,
and how much. I told him the whole truth. 'Three bushels of
wheat,' I said, 'six of barley, the same of millet, but only four
quarts of beans: they did not thrive this year. You take the wheat
and barley,' said I, 'and leave us the millet. But if you need
millet take that too.' 'Don't you make any wine?' another man
asked. 'We do,' I said; 'if any of you comes we shall let him have
it. But be sure to bring a wineskin, for we haven't any.' 'How
many vines have you?' 'Two,' said I, 'at the house door, twenty
inside the yard, and the same number on the other side of the
creek, which we lately set out. They are very fine and produce
big clusters, when passers-by let them be. But to save you the
trouble of asking item by item I shall tell you what else we have:
eight she-goats, a mulley cow, her pretty calf, four sickles, four
hoes, three spears, and each of us has a knife for hunting. For
crockery . . . But why speak of that? We have wives and children.
We live in two fine huts, and there is a third for storing the grain
and the skins.' 'Yes, by Zeus,' the speaker said, 'and for burying
your money, too, belike.' 'Then go and dig it up, fool. Who
buries money? It doesn't grow, you know.' Here everybody
laughed, and I thought it was him they were laughing at.

" 'That is what we have. If you want all of it we will give it
you for the asking: you don't have to seize it from us as if we
were foreigners or wicked folk unwilling to give it up. We, too,
mark you, are citizens of this city, as my father used to say. Once
when he came here there was a distribution of cash bonuses to
citizens, and he got his with the rest. Our children, too, we are
raising to be your fellow citizens, and if you are ever in need
they will help you, against robbers or enemies. Now, of course,
there is peace; but if such an emergency should arise you will
pray for more like us to show up. Don't imagine that this
speaker here will ever fight for you; he can scold, of course, like a
woman. We will give you a share of meat and hides when we
catch any game: just send someone to fetch them. If you bid us
pull our huts down we shall pull them down if they harm you.
But then give us housing here: else how can we endure this

winter? There are plenty of houses inside your walls which no one lives in; one of them will be enough for us. But if we do not live here, if we do not add to the congestion of so many people living in the same spot, does that make us candidates for resettlement?'

" 'Now that ungodly and wicked business of shipwrecks he brazenly spoke of—I almost forgot to mention it, though it should have been my first point—could any of you possibly believe it? To say nothing of the immorality, not a thing can be salvaged in that place. All the timbers you can see are splinters; nothing bigger is ever cast up. The beach, morever, is the most inaccessible in the world. I did once find oars which had been cast up, but them I nailed to the sacred oak by the sea. Heaven forbid that I should ever get profit or gain from people's misfortune! No, I have received no benefits whatever from shipwrecks, but have often pitied their mariners when they came my way. I have received them in my hut, have given them food and drink, helped them in any other way I could, and escorted them back to civilization. But which of them would bear me witness now? It was not for testimonials or gratitude that I helped those people—I never even knew where they came from. I only hope that none of you is ever involved in that kind of experience.'

"While I was making my speech a man in the audience arose, and I thought to myself, 'There was another of the same ilk, doubtless ready to lie about me.' But this is what he said: 'Gentlemen, I have long been in two minds about this man. I could not believe he was the man I thought, but now I am positive that he is. It would be criminal, or worse, sinful, not to declare what I know and render payment in mere words for the substantial acts of kindness I experienced. I am, as you are aware, a citizen,' he continued, and, pointing to his neighbor who then also rose from his seat, said, 'and so is this man. Two years ago it happened that we were sailing in Socles' boat. The boat was wrecked off Caphereus, with the loss of all but very few of its passengers. Of these some were taken in by purple fishers, for they had money in their purses. But we were stripped bare when we were cast up, and so walked along a track hoping to find some shepherds' or cowherds' shelter. We might have died of hunger and thirst, but after a struggle got to some huts, where we stopped and called for help. This man came up and brought us in and kindled a slow fire, which he increased by degrees. He himself rubbed one of us down and his wife the other—with lard, for they had no oil. Finally they poured warm water over us until they brought us round; we had been numb with cold. Then they made us lie down, covered us with what they had, and put wheat loaves before us to eat. They themselves ate parched millet, and they gave us wine to drink while they themselves drank water. Venison was plentiful, both roasted and boiled. The next day we wanted to leave, but they kept us for three days. Then they saw us down to the plain, and when we left gave us meat and a very fine skin for each of us. When he noticed that my health was still delicate from my recent exposure, he put a little tunic on me which he took off his daughter; she wrapped another rag round herself. When we got to a village I gave the tunic back. Next after the gods, then, it is due to this man that we have survived.'

"The people had listened to the man's speech with pleasure and they applauded me. Now I recollected the incident. I called out, 'Hello, Sotades!' I went up and kissed him and the other man. When I did so the people laughed heartily, and then I realized that in the cities people do not kiss one another. Then that kindly man who had spoken for me in the beginning came forward and said, 'I propose, gentlemen, that we invite this man to dine in the town hall. If he had saved one of our citizens by shielding him in war he would have obtained many fine gifts. Now he has saved two citizens, and perhaps others who are not here: does he deserve no reward at all? In return for the tunic which he stripped from his daughter to give to our citizen in distress, the city ought to give him a cloak as well as a tunic. This would serve as an encouragement to others to be righteous and help one another. The free use of the farm should be voted to these men and their children, and no one must trouble them. Furthermore the man should be given a hundred drachmas for tools: this sum I offer from my own funds on behalf of the city.' For this offer he was applauded, and his other proposals were carried out. The clothes and the money were brought to the theater at once. I didn't wish to accept them, but they said, 'You can't dine in the skin!' 'Well, then,' said I, 'I shall go dinnerless today.' They put the tunic on notwithstanding, and threw the cloak over my shoulders. I wanted to throw my skin on top, but they wouldn't let me. The money they could not force upon me; I swore I would not take it. 'If you are looking for someone who will take it,' said I, 'give it to that orator and let him bury it; he is obviously expert in the business.' From that time on no one has molested us."

He had hardly finished his tale when we arrived at the huts. I said with a smile, "One thing you kept hidden from your fellow citizens, and it is the finest possession of all." "What is that?" said he. "This garden," I said, "it is very pretty and has many vegetables and trees." "It wasn't here then," he said; "we made it later." Then we went in and spent the rest of the day feasting. We reclined on a mattress of leaves and skins piled high, and the wife sat near her husband. A daughter of marriageable age waited on us and poured us a sweet dark wine to drink. The boys prepared the meat, and they themselves dined as they served. I felicitated those people and thought their life blessed beyond any I knew. And yet I knew the houses and tables of the rich, and not of private individuals only, but of vice-regents and kings. Those latter I had always thought wretched, but particularly so when I saw liberty combined with poverty in that hut. Not even in the pleasures of food and drink did they fall short; even here they had something of an advantage.

We had already made ourselves quite comfortable when that other man came, and with him his son, not a bad-looking lad, carrying a hare. The boy blushed when he came in, and while his father was greeting us he kissed the girl and gave her the hare. The girl then stopped serving and sat down by her mother, and the lad served in her place. "Is she the one," I asked my host, "whose tunic you took off and gave to the ship-wrecked mariner?" "No," he said with a laugh, "she was married off long ago, to a rich man in the village; she now has big children." "They surely supply any needs you may have?" said I. "We have no needs," said the woman; "*they* get game from us when we have any, and fruit and vegetables, for they have no garden. Last year we got some wheat from them for seed, but we gave it back at the beginning of harvest." "How about this one," said I; "do you plan to marry her to a rich man, so she too can lend you wheat?" At that both blushed, the girl as well as the boy. "She will get a poor man to husband," said her father, "a hunter like ourselves." He glanced at the young man with a smile and I said, "But why aren't you marrying her at once? Must the man come from some village?" "It's no long way, I think; actually he is in the house. We shall make the marriage when we have chosen a good day." "How do you judge whether a day is good?" said I. "When the moon is not in a quarter," he said. "The air must be pure too, and the weather bright." "Is the lad really a good hunter?" said I. "I am indeed," the young fellow interposed. "I can wear down a deer and face a boar's charge. You shall see tomorrow if you like, stranger." "And did you catch this hare?" I asked. "I did," he said, laughing. "With my net, during the night. The weather was very clear and the moon bigger than it had ever been." The two men laughed, not only the girl's father but the boy's too. But he was ashamed and fell silent.

Now the girl's father spoke up. "It is not I that am putting you off, my boy," he said. "Your own father is waiting until he can go buy a victim; we must sacrifice to the gods, you know." Here the girl's younger brother interposed. "A victim? He got one ready long ago. It is fattening under cover behind the hut; it's a fine animal." They asked the swain, "Really true?" And when he said it was they asked, "Where did you get it?" "When we caught the sow that had the litter," he said. "All but one got away; they were quicker than the hare. One I hit with a stone, threw my jacket over it, and caught it. I swapped it for a piglet in the village, made a sty for it behind the house, and raised it." "So that is why your mother smiled when I wondered at hearing a pig grunt, and that's why you were so extravagant with barley." "The chestnuts were not enough to fatten her, even if she would be satisfied with only nuts. But if you would like to see her I will go bring her." They told him to do so, and he and the boys scampered off elated. Meanwhile the girl had got up and fetched from the other hut sliced sorb apples, medlars, winter apples, and swelling clusters of fine grapes. She wiped the stains of the meat off the table, spread some clean fern on it, and put her fruit on it. The boys came in with the pig, laughing and frolicking. After them came the swain's mother and two little brothers. They brought new loaves, boiled eggs on wooden slabs, and roasted chick-peas.

When she had greeted her brother and niece, the boy's mother sat down by her husband and said, "There is the victim, which the boy has been feeding for his wedding, and everything else is ready on our side. The barley and wheat have been ground. All we may need is a little more wine, and it's no trouble to get that from the village." Close beside her stood her son, looking to his father-in-law. The latter smiled and said, "*He* is the one who is holding things up. Maybe he wants to get the pig fatter." "Why she is ready to burst with fat," said the lad. I wanted to help him out and said, "Take care; while the pig grows fat its master may grow lean." "Our guest is quite right," said his mother. "Even now he is thinner than himself. And the other day I noticed he couldn't sleep at night, and went out of the hut." "The dogs were barking," said the boy, "and I went out to look around." "Not you," said she; "you were rambling around distracted. Let's not torture him any longer." She embraced and kissed the girl's mother, who turned to her husband and said, "Let us do as they wish." It was so decided, and they fixed the wedding for the third day. They also invited me to stay for the occasion, and I did so very willingly.

The Library of Liberal Arts

The American Heritage Series